MEDITERRANEAN DIET HEALTHY DIS

QUICK BREAKFASTS
MINI FRITTATAS WITH SPINACH AND FETA	3
GREEK YOGURT PARFAIT	4
MEDITERRANEAN AVOCADO TOAST	5
BANANA AND NUT BUTTER ROLL-UPS	6
QUICK SHAKSHUKA	7
COTTAGE CHEESE WITH PISTACHIOS AND HONEY	8

SNACKS AND SIDES
CLASSIC HUMMUS WITH VEGGIE STICKS	9
CAPRESE SKEWERS	10
OLIVE TAPENADE ON CROSTINI	11
GREEK YOGURT TZATZIKI WITH CUCUMBERS	12
STUFFED DATES WITH ALMOND	13
QUICK MARINATED OLIVES	14

SIMPLE SALADS
SPEEDY GREEK SALAD	15
ARUGULA AND WATERMELON SALAD	16
MEDITERRANEAN CHICKPEA SALAD	17
CUCUMBER AND FETA SALAD	18
QUINOA TABBOULEH	19
SPINACH AND AVOCADO SALAD	20

SPEEDY SANDWICHES AND WRAPS
TURKEY AND HUMMUS WRAP	21
GRILLED VEGETABLE PITA	22
TUNA AND OLIVE TAPENADE SANDWICH	23
EGGPLANT AND ROASTED PEPPER WRAP	24
MEDITERRANEAN CHICKEN PITA	25
FALAFEL WRAP WITH TAHINI SAUCE	26

EXPRESS PASTA AND GRAINS
TOMATO BASIL PASTA	27
LEMON GARLIC COUSCOUS	28
SPINACH AND FETA ORZO	29
QUICK PESTO ZOODLES	30
SAUTÉED SHRIMP OVER QUINOA	31
MEDITERRANEAN RICE SALAD	32

FAST FISH AND SEAFOOD
GARLIC LEMON SHRIMP	33
SEARED TUNA SALAD	34
MEDITERRANEAN MACKEREL TOAST	35
SALMON WITH DILL YOGURT SAUCE	36
QUICK SARDINE PASTA	37
GRILLED OCTOPUS SALAD	38

VEGETARIAN DELIGHTS
CHICKPEA AND AVOCADO MASH	39
STUFFED MINI BELL PEPPERS	40
ZUCCHINI RIBBON SALAD	41
QUICK EGGPLANT PARMESAN	42
GARLIC AND HERB ROASTED CAULIFLOWER	43

MEATS IN MINUTES
LEMON HERB CHICKEN CUTLETS	44
BEEF AND ARUGULA PITA POCKETS	45
QUICK LAMB KOFTA	46
MEDITERRANEAN TURKEY MEATBALLS	47
PORK TENDERLOIN MEDALLIONS WITH OLIVES	48
CHICKEN SOUVLAKI SKEWERS	49

NO-COOK DISHES
MEDITERRANEAN CHEESE AND CHARCUTERIE BOARD	50
AVOCADO AND CRAB SALAD	51
PROSCIUTTO AND MELON PLATTER	52
SMOKED SALMON AND CREAM CHEESE CUCUMBER BITES	53
CHICKPEA AND ROASTED PEPPER DIP	54
GREEK YOGOURT AND FRUIT CUPS	55
TOMATO AND MOZZARELLA CAPRESE	56

DESSERTS AND SWEET TREATS
GREEK YOGURT WITH HONEY AND WALNUTS	57
CHOCOLATE-DIPPED FIGS	58
ORANGE AND ALMOND SALAD	59
QUICK BERRY SORBET	60
PISTACHIO AND APRICOT BITES	61
RICOTTA AND BERRY PARFAIT	62

MEDITERRANEAN MEAL PREP	63
THE MEDITERRANEAN CALENDAR	64
STRESS REDUCTION TO WELLBEING	65
90 DAY MEAL PLAN	66

MEDITERRAENAN DIET DISHES IN 10 MINUTES

Quick Breakfasts: A Vibrant Start
Begin your day with a burst of Mediterranean sunshine through recipes that are as nutritious as they are easy to prepare. **Mini Frittatas with Spinach and Feta, Greek Yogurt Parfait,** and **Mediterranean Avocado Toast** offer a perfect balance of protein, healthy fats, and carbohydrates to energize your morning. These dishes are designed for busy mornings, ensuring that even the most time-pressed individuals can enjoy a wholesome start to their day.

Snacks and Sides: Flavorful Interludes
The Mediterranean diet shines in its approach to snacking, transforming it from a guilty pleasure into an opportunity to nourish your body. Explore a variety of snacks and sides that are both satisfying and healthful, such as **Classic Hummus with Veggie Sticks, Caprese Skewers,** and **Olive Tapenade on Crostini**. These recipes are not only quick to prepare but also packed with flavors and nutrients, making them perfect for mid-day treats or appetizing sides.

Simple Salads and Speedy Sandwiches and Wraps: The Heart of Mediterranean
Salads, sandwiches, and wraps form the backbone of Mediterranean lunchtime cuisine, offering a perfect showcase for the region's fresh produce and vibrant flavors. From the simplicity of a **Speedy Greek Salad** to the creativity of a **Falafel Wrap with Tahini Sauce**, these recipes are designed for convenience without compromising on taste or nutrition. They embody the diet's principles of freshness and simplicity, ensuring that a nutritious meal is always within easy reach.

Meats in Minutes and Fast Fish and Seafood: Protein-Rich Delights
Lean meats and seafood are integral to the Mediterranean diet, providing essential proteins and omega-3 fatty acids. This cookbook offers a plethora of options for incorporating these healthy proteins into your diet, from **Quick Lamb Kofta** and **Mediterranean Turkey Meatballs** to **Seared Tuna Salad** and **Salmon with Dill Yogurt Sauce**. Each recipe is crafted to be straightforward and quick, making it possible to enjoy a protein-rich, flavorful meal any night of the week.

Express Pasta and Grains: The Soul of Mediterranean Cuisine
Pasta and grains hold a special place in Mediterranean cooking, serving as the foundation for many iconic dishes. This section introduces you to quick and nutritious recipes like **Tomato Basil Pasta, Lemon Garlic Couscous,** and **Quick Pesto Zoodles**, which are not only satisfying but also embody the diet's emphasis on whole grains and fresh ingredients. These dishes are perfect for busy weeknights, offering comfort and nutrition in equal measure.

Vegetarian Delights and No-Cook Dishes: Effortless Eating
For those seeking to incorporate more plant-based meals into their diets or looking for no-fuss recipes, this section is a treasure trove of inspiration. From **Chickpea and Avocado Mash** to **Tomato and Mozzarella Caprese** and **Lemon Garlic Couscous**, these recipes celebrate the abundance and variety of vegetables in the Mediterranean diet. They are quick, easy, and require minimal cooking, making healthy eating accessible and enjoyable.

Desserts and Sweet Treats: A Wholesome Indulgence
The Mediterranean approach to sweets is one of moderation, focusing on natural ingredients and fruits. Indulge in healthier dessert options like **Chocolate-Dipped Figs, Quick Berry Sorbet,** and **Ricotta and Berry Parfait**, which satisfy sweet cravings without the guilt. These recipes showcase the natural sweetness of fruits, complemented by nuts and honey, reflecting the diet's overall philosophy of balance and wholesomeness.

Mini Frittatas with Spinach and Feta

1. **(Preheat Oven) (1 minute)**: Begin by preheating your oven to 350°F (175°C). This initial step ensures that the oven reaches the perfect temperature for baking the frittatas efficiently.
2. **(Prepare Ingredients) (2 minutes)**: Chop the spinach finely and crumble the feta cheese. Lightly beat the eggs in a bowl. These preparations ensure that your ingredients blend smoothly.
3. **(Combine Ingredients) (2 minutes)**: Mix the eggs, spinach, and feta cheese in a bowl. Season with salt and pepper to taste. The combination of these ingredients will form the base of your frittatas.
4. **(Cook on Stovetop) (3 minutes)**: Heat olive oil in a non-stick pan over medium heat. Pour the mixture into the pan to form small frittatas. Cook until the edges start to set.
5. **(Finish in Oven) (2 minutes)**: Transfer the pan to the oven and bake for 2 minutes or until the frittatas are fully set. This final step ensures a delightful texture.

INGREDIENTS

- 4 large eggs (120g or ~4.2 oz)
- 1 cup spinach, chopped (30g or ~1 oz)
- 1/3 cup feta cheese, crumbled (50g or ~1.75 oz)
- 2 teaspoons olive oil (10ml)

NUTRITION

- **Kcal per serve:** 400 kcal
- **Carbohydrates:** Approx. 3g
- **Protein:** Approx. 22g
- **Total Fats:** Approx. 33g
- **Saturated Fats:** Approx. 10g
- **Monounsaturated Fats:** Approx. 15g
- **Polyunsaturated Fats:** Approx. 3g
- **Sodium:** Approx. 600mg

Greek Yogurt Parfait

1. **(Gather Ingredients) (1 minute):** Start by collecting all ingredients. This simplifies the process, ensuring everything is at hand.
2. **(Layer Greek Yogurt) (2 minutes):** Spoon half the Greek yogurt into two glasses. Layering creates the parfait's base.
3. **(Add Berries) (2 minutes):** Divide half the mixed berries between glasses. Their vibrant colors add appeal.
4. **(Sprinkle Granola) (2 minutes):** Add a layer of granola for crunch. Its texture contrasts the creamy yogurt.
5. **(Top with Honey) (2 minutes):** Drizzle honey over each parfait. Finish with the remaining yogurt, berries, and a granola sprinkle.

INGREDIENTS

- 6 oz (175g) Greek Yogurt
- 1.5 oz (45g) Granola
- 0.5 oz (15g) Honey
- 3.5 oz (100g) Mixed Berries

NUTRITION

- **Kcal per serve:** 400 kcal
- **Carbohydrates:** Approx. 50g
- **Protein:** Approx. 20g
- **Total Fats:** Approx. 10g
- **Saturated Fats:** Approx. 2g
- **Monounsaturated Fats:** Approx. 2.5g
- **Polyunsaturated Fats:** Approx. 3.5g
- **Sodium:** Approx. 100mg

Mediterranean Avocado Toast

1. **(Prepare the Ingredients) (2 minutes):** Toast the whole grain bread slices to your desired crispiness. Slice the avocado and cherry tomatoes. Crumble the feta cheese.
2. **(Assemble the Avocado) (2 minutes):** Spread the avocado evenly on each slice of toast. Use a fork to mash it slightly.
3. **(Add Tomatoes and Feta) (2 minutes):** Top the mashed avocado with cherry tomatoes and crumbled feta cheese, distributing them evenly over both slices.
4. **(Drizzle and Season) (2 minutes):** Drizzle olive oil and squeeze lemon juice over the top. Add a pinch of salt and pepper to taste.
5. **(Serve) (2 minutes):** Place the prepared avocado toast on plates. Garnish with any remaining herbs or spices you prefer for an extra flavor boost.

INGREDIENTS

- 2 slices (80g) Whole Grain Bread
- 1/2 (100g) Avocado
- 1/2 cup (75g) Cherry Tomatoes
- 1 oz (30g) Feta Cheese
- 1 tsp (5ml) Olive Oil
- 2 tsp (10ml) Lemon Juice

NUTRITION

- **Kcal per serve:** 400 kcal
- **Carbohydrates:** Approx. 3g
- **Protein:** Approx. 22g
- **Total Fats:** Approx. 33g
- **Saturated Fats:** Approx. 10g
- **Monounsaturated Fats:** Approx. 15g
- **Polyunsaturated Fats:** Approx. 3g
- **Sodium:** Approx. 600mg

Banana and Nut Butter Roll-Ups

1. **(Gather Ingredients) (1 minute):** Start by assembling your whole grain tortillas, ripe bananas, and your choice of nut butter.
2. **(Spread Nut Butter) (2 minutes):** Evenly spread 1 tablespoon of nut butter over each tortilla, covering the surface to the edges.
3. **(Add Banana) (2 minutes):** Place a whole banana on each tortilla, positioning it near the edge to facilitate rolling.
4. **(Roll Tortillas) (2 minutes):** Carefully roll the tortilla around the banana, ensuring the nut butter acts as a 'glue' to hold the roll-up together.
5. **(Serve) (2 minutes):** Cut each roll-up in half, if desired, and serve immediately for a quick, nutritious meal.

INGREDIENTS

- 2 Whole Grain Tortillas (2 x 50g)
- 2 Bananas (2 x 115g)
- 2 tbsp Nut Butter (30g)

NUTRITION

- **Kcal per serve:** 300 kcal
- **Carbohydrates:** 47.45g
- **Protein:** 8.02g
- **Total Fats:** 11.34g
- **Saturated Fats:** 2.12g
- **Monounsaturated Fats:** 4.6g
- **Polyunsaturated Fats:** 3.72g
- **Sodium:** 227.05mg

Quick Shakshuka

1. **(Prep Ingredients) (2 minutes):** Begin by finely chopping the onion and bell pepper. Open the can of tomatoes. Measure out your spices, having cumin, paprika, and a pinch of salt and pepper ready. This prep work streamlines the cooking process.
2. **(Cook Onion and Pepper) (3 minutes):** In a large skillet, heat the olive oil over medium heat. Add the chopped onion and bell pepper, sautéing until they start to soften and turn golden. The aroma should be enticing and vegetables tender.
3. **(Add Tomatoes and Spices) (2 minutes):** Pour the canned tomatoes into the skillet with the sautéed vegetables. Stir in the spices evenly. Let the mixture simmer for a minute, allowing the flavors to meld together. The sauce should start to thicken slightly.
4. **(Crack Eggs into Sauce) (2 minutes):** Make four small wells in the sauce with a spoon. Crack an egg into each well. It's crucial not to stir so the eggs can poach directly in the tomato sauce, retaining their shape.
5. **(Cover and Cook Eggs) (4 minutes):** Reduce the heat to low. Cover the skillet with a lid or aluminum foil. Let the eggs cook until the whites are set but the yolks remain runny. Watching the eggs closely ensures they don't overcook.
6. **(Garnish and Serve) (2 minutes):** Once the eggs are cooked to your liking, season the shakshuka with a final pinch of salt and pepper. Garnish with chopped fresh herbs like cilantro or parsley if desired. Serve hot, directly from the skillet, with crusty bread on the side for dipping.

INGREDIENTS

- 14 oz (400g) Canned Tomatoes
- 4 Eggs (200g)
- 1 tbsp (15ml) Olive Oil
- 3.5 oz (100g) Onion
- 3.5 oz (100g) Bell Pepper
- 1 tsp (5g) Spices (cumin, paprika)

NUTRITION

- **Kcal per serve:** 300 kcal
- **Carbohydrates:** 48g
- **Protein:** 8g
- **Total Fats:** 12g
- **Saturated Fats:** 2g
- **Monounsaturated Fats:** 5g
- **Polyunsaturated Fats:** 4g
- **Sodium:** 230mg

Cottage Cheese with Pistachios and Honey

1. **(Prepare Ingredients) (1 minute)**: Measure out the cottage cheese into two bowls. Roughly chop the pistachios if they are not already in small pieces. Have your honey ready for drizzling.
2. **(Add Pistachios) (1 minute)**: Sprinkle the chopped pistachios evenly over the bowls of cottage cheese, dividing them equally between the servings.
3. **(Drizzle Honey) (1 minute)**: Carefully drizzle honey over the cottage cheese and pistachios in each bowl. The honey adds a touch of sweetness that complements the creamy texture of the cheese and the crunch of the nuts.
4. **(Garnish) (1 minute)**: Optionally, garnish with a few whole pistachios or a sprinkle of ground cinnamon for an extra layer of flavor and presentation.
5. **(Serve) (1 minute)**: Serve immediately while fresh. This dish can be enjoyed as a nutritious breakfast, a quick snack, or a light dessert.

INGREDIENTS

- 1 1/2 cups (300g) Cottage Cheese
- 1/4 cup (30g) Pistachios, shelled and unsalted
- 2 tbsp (40g) Honey

NUTRITION

- **Kcal per serve:** 300 kcal
- **Carbohydrates:** 26g
- **Protein:** 20g
- **Total Fats:** 13g
- **Saturated Fats:** 3.4g
- **Monounsaturated Fats:** 5.1g
- **Polyunsaturated Fats:** 2.4g
- **Sodium:** 547mg

Classic Hummus with Veggie Sticks

1. **(Blend Chickpeas) (2 minutes):** In a food processor, blend the cooked chickpeas until smooth, adding a bit of water if necessary to achieve a creamy consistency.
2. **(Add Tahini and Olive Oil) (2 minutes):** Incorporate tahini and olive oil into the chickpea mixture, blending until the mixture is well combined and smooth.
3. **(Season) (1 minute):** Add minced garlic and lemon juice to the hummus. Blend again. Taste and adjust seasoning with salt and pepper as desired.
4. **(Prepare Veggie Sticks)** (2 minutes): While the hummus is blending, slice the vegetables into sticks for dipping. Choose a variety of colors and textures for appeal and nutrition.
5. **(Serve) (3 minutes):** Spoon the hummus into a serving bowl. Drizzle with a little more olive oil, if desired, and serve with the veggie sticks on the side for dipping.

INGREDIENTS

- 7 oz (200g) Cooked Chickpeas
- 1 oz (30g) Tahini
- 1 tbsp (15ml) Olive Oil
- 4 tsp (20ml) Lemon Juice
- 2 cloves (10g) Garlic
- 7 oz (200g) Mixed Vegetables (carrots, cucumbers, bell peppers)

NUTRITION

- **Kcal per serve:** 400 kcal
- **Carbohydrates:** 38g
- **Protein:** 12g
- **Total Fats:** 22g
- **Saturated Fats:** 3g
- **Monounsaturated Fats:** 11g
- **Polyunsaturated Fats:** 8g
- **Sodium:** 200mg

Caprese Skewers

1. **(Gather Ingredients) (2 minutes):** Begin by washing the cherry tomatoes and basil leaves under cold water. Pat them dry with a paper towel. Collect the mozzarella cheese balls from their brine and let them drain. Measure out the olive oil and balsamic glaze.
2. **(Assemble Skewers) (3 minutes):** Start threading the ingredients onto the skewers. Begin with a cherry tomato, then a basil leaf folded in half, followed by a mozzarella ball. Repeat the process until the skewer is filled. Make sure to leave a little space at the end for handling.
3. **(Arrange on Platter) (1 minute):** Carefully arrange the completed skewers on a large serving platter. Try to lay them out neatly in rows or a pattern that showcases the colors and makes them easy to pick up.
4. **(Drizzle Olive Oil and Balsamic Glaze) (2 minutes):** Drizzle olive oil over the skewers, ensuring each one gets a little coating. Then, artistically drizzle the balsamic glaze across the skewers. The glaze should add a beautiful shine and an extra layer of flavor.
5. **(Final Touches) (2 minutes):** Give a final check to ensure each skewer looks appetizing. You might sprinkle a little sea salt or cracked black pepper over them for an extra flavor kick. Now, your Caprese Skewers are ready to be enjoyed. Serve them immediately for the freshest taste.

INGREDIENTS

- 7 oz (200g) Cherry Tomatoes
- 3.5 oz (100g) Mozzarella Cheese (fresh, small balls)
- 0.7 oz (20g) Basil Leaves
- 1 tbsp (15ml) Olive Oil
- 2 tsp (10ml) Balsamic Glaze

NUTRITION

- **Kcal per serve:** 400 kcal
- **Carbohydrates:** 8g
- **Protein:** 15g
- **Total Fats:** 32g
- **Saturated Fats:** 12g
- **Monounsaturated Fats:** 16g
- **Polyunsaturated Fats:** 2g
- **Sodium:** 386mg

Olive Tapenade on Crostini

1. **(Ingredient Preparation) (2 minutes):** Begin by finely chopping the olives, capers, and garlic clove. This mixture will form the base of your tapenade, providing a rich blend of flavors that complement each other perfectly in every bite.
2. **(Making the Tapenade) (2 minutes):** Combine the chopped ingredients in a mixing bowl. Add half of the olive oil and mix thoroughly. The consistency should be spreadable but still slightly chunky, allowing the individual flavors to stand out.
3. **(Toasting the Baguette) (2 minutes):** Slice the baguette into thin pieces. Brush each slice lightly with the remaining olive oil. Toast them until golden and crisp. This will be your crostini base, providing a delightful crunch that pairs well with the creamy tapenade.
4. **(Assembly) (2 minutes):** Spread a generous layer of olive tapenade on each crostini. The tapenade's savory flavor, combined with the crostini's crispness, creates a perfect balance. Arrange the crostini on a serving platter in a visually appealing manner.
5. **(Final Touches) (2 minutes):** Garnish each tapenade-topped crostini with a small basil leaf or a drizzle of balsamic reduction for an extra layer of flavor and elegance. Serve immediately, allowing guests to enjoy the freshness of this Mediterranean delight.

INGREDIENTS

- 3.5 oz (100g) Baguette, sliced and toasted
- 1.75 oz (50g) Olives, pitted
- 0.35 oz (10g) Capers
- 1 clove (5g) Garlic
- 4 tsp (20ml) Olive Oil

NUTRITION

- **Kcal per serve:** 325 kcal
- **Carbohydrates:** 33g
- **Protein:** 6g
- **Total Fats:** 19g
- **Saturated Fats:** 3g
- **Monounsaturated Fats:** 13g
- **Polyunsaturated Fats:** 2g
- **Sodium:** 568mg

Greek Yogurt Tzatziki with Cucumbers

1. **(Grate Cucumber) (2 minutes):** Peel and grate the cucumber. Squeeze out the excess water using a clean cloth or paper towel. This process ensures the tzatziki sauce remains thick and not watered down.
2. **(Combine Ingredients) (2 minutes):** In a bowl, mix the Greek yogurt with the grated cucumber, minced garlic, lemon juice, and chopped dill. Stir until all components are evenly distributed throughout the yogurt.
3. **(Season) (1 minute):** Add olive oil to the mixture for richness. Season with salt and pepper to taste. The olive oil not only adds flavor but also contributes to the creamy texture of the tzatziki.
4. **(Chill) (1 minute):** For the best flavor, let the tzatziki chill in the refrigerator for a few minutes before serving. This step allows the flavors to meld together.
5. **(Serve) (4 minutes):** Serve the tzatziki in a small bowl, garnished with a drizzle of olive oil and a sprinkle of dill. Pair with fresh cucumber slices or your choice of vegetables for dipping.

INGREDIENTS

- 1 1/4 cups (300g) Greek Yogurt
- 3.5 oz (100g) Cucumber, deseeded and grated
- 1 clove (5g) Garlic, minced
- 1 tbsp (15ml) Lemon Juice
- 1 tsp (5g) Dill, chopped
- 2 tsp (10ml) Olive Oil

NUTRITION

- **Kcal per serve:** 236 kcal
- **Carbohydrates:** 9g
- **Protein:** 16g
- **Total Fats:** 16g
- **Saturated Fats:** 2g
- **Monounsaturated Fats:** 11g
- **Polyunsaturated Fats:** 2g
- **Sodium:** 57mg

Stuffed Dates with Almond

1. **(Prepare Dates) (2 minutes):** Carefully slit each date on one side and remove the pit. This creates a cavity for the almond, ensuring the date retains its shape while allowing space for stuffing.
2. **(Stuff Dates) (3 minutes):** Insert an almond into the cavity of each date. Press the date gently to close around the almond, ensuring it is snugly fitted inside. The contrast in textures between the soft date and the crunchy almond is delightful.
3. **(Arrange for Serving) (2 minutes):** Place the stuffed dates on a serving plate in a single layer. The presentation is key, so take a moment to arrange them neatly, showcasing their natural beauty and the care taken in preparation.
4. **(Garnish) (2 minutes):** Optionally, drizzle a little honey over the stuffed dates or sprinkle them with powdered sugar for an extra touch of sweetness. This step enhances the flavors and adds a visual appeal to the dish.
5. **(Serve) (1 minute):** Serve the stuffed dates immediately as a sweet and nutritious snack or dessert. They are perfect for sharing and offer a burst of energy and flavor with each bite.

INGREDIENTS

- **10-12 Dates** (3.5 oz or 100g)
- **25 Almonds** (1.75 oz or 50g)

NUTRITION

- Kcal per serve: 283 kcal
- Carbohydrates: 43g
- Protein: 6g
- Total Fats: 13g
- Saturated Fats: 1g
- Monounsaturated Fats: 8g
- Polyunsaturated Fats: 3g
- Sodium: 1mg

Quick Marinated Olives

1. **Mixing the Marinade (2 minutes)**: Combine olive oil, minced garlic, lemon juice, and mixed herbs in a bowl. Stir thoroughly to blend the flavors, ensuring the garlic is well distributed within the mixture for an even taste throughout the olives.
2. **Adding Olives (1 minute)**: Add the olives to the bowl with the marinade. Gently toss the olives until they are fully coated with the marinade. This step is crucial for infusing the olives with the aromatic flavors of the garlic, lemon, and herbs.
3. **Marinating (5 minutes)**: Let the olives marinate at room temperature. During this time, the olives will start to absorb the flavors of the marinade, becoming more aromatic and flavorful. This short marination period is perfect for a quick preparation.
4. **Serving Preparation (1 minute)**: Prepare a serving dish or bowl. Use a slotted spoon to transfer the marinated olives from the bowl to the serving dish, allowing excess marinade to drip off. This ensures the olives are well-presented and not overly oily.
5. **Final Touches (1 minute)**: Drizzle a small amount of the marinade over the olives in the serving dish. This step enhances the presentation and flavor of the dish, giving it a glossy finish and a burst of flavor from the marinade.

INGREDIENTS

- 7 oz (200 g) Olives
- 1 oz (30 ml) Olive Oil
- 0.7 oz (20 g) Garlic, minced
- 1.4 oz (40 ml) Lemon Juice
- 1 tsp (5 g) Mixed Herbs (such as thyme and oregano)

NUTRITION

- **Kcal**: 400
- **Carbohydrates**: 12 g
- **Protein**: 1.6 g
- **Total Fats**: 40 g
- **Saturated Fats**: 5.6 g
- **Monounsaturated Fats**: 29.5 g
- **Polyunsaturated Fats**: 4.8 g
- **Sodium**: 1470 mg

Speedy Greek Salad

1. **Chop Vegetables (2 minutes)**: Begin by dicing the tomatoes, cucumber, and red onion into bite-sized pieces. Ensure each piece is evenly cut to enhance the salad's visual appeal and ensure a uniform distribution of flavors in every bite.
2. **Crumble Feta (1 minute)**: Take the block of feta cheese and crumble it into small, bite-sized pieces over a bowl. The goal is to distribute the cheese evenly throughout the salad, adding a creamy texture and rich flavor that complements the fresh vegetables.
3. **Mix Ingredients (2 minutes)**: In a large salad bowl, combine the chopped vegetables, crumbled feta cheese, and olives. Gently toss the ingredients to ensure a good mix, allowing the varied textures and flavors to meld together harmoniously.
4. **Prepare Dressing (2 minutes)**: In a small bowl, whisk together the olive oil and lemon juice until well combined. This simple dressing will add a bright, tangy flavor that enhances the natural taste of the salad ingredients.
5. **Dress and Serve (3 minutes)**: Drizzle the dressing over the salad and toss it lightly to ensure all ingredients are coated evenly. Serve immediately to enjoy the salad at its freshest, with the dressing adding a zesty finish to the crisp vegetables and salty feta.

INGREDIENTS

- 7.oz (203 g) Tomatoes
- 3.5 oz (102 g) Cucumber
- 2 oz (56 g) Red Onion
- 5 oz (142 g) Feta Cheese
- 2.5 oz (68 g) Olives
- 1 oz (30 ml) Olive Oil
- 1 oz (24 ml) Lemon Juice

NUTRITION

- **Kcal**: 400
- **Carbohydrates**: 14 g
- **Protein**: 8 g
- **Total Fats**: 34 g
- **Saturated Fats**: 14 g
- **Monounsaturated Fats**: 15 g
- **Polyunsaturated Fats**: 5 g
- **Sodium**: 1155 mg

Arugula and Watermelon Salad

1. **Prepare the Base (2 minutes)**: Arrange the arugula leaves evenly on two plates. This leafy green serves as the bed for the salad, providing a peppery base that contrasts beautifully with the sweet watermelon and salty feta cheese.
2. **Add Watermelon (2 minutes)**: Distribute the cubed watermelon over the arugula. The juicy, sweet cubes add a refreshing element to the salad, making it perfect for a summer meal or a light, refreshing side.
3. **Crumble Feta (1 minute)**: Sprinkle crumbled feta cheese over the watermelon and arugula. The cheese adds a creamy texture and a sharp, salty flavor that balances the sweetness of the watermelon.
4. **Dress the Salad (2 minutes)**: Whisk together balsamic vinegar and olive oil in a small bowl. Drizzle this dressing over the salad, adding a tangy and rich flavor that ties all the ingredients together.
5. **Final Touches (3 minutes)**: Gently toss the salad on each plate to mix the dressing with the arugula, watermelon, and feta. Serve immediately to enjoy the salad at its peak freshness and flavor.

INGREDIENTS

- 2 oz (55 g) Arugula
- 11 oz (306 g) Watermelon, cubed
- 5 oz (150 g) Feta Cheese, crumbled
- 1 oz (37 ml) Balsamic Vinegar
- 1 oz (30 ml) Olive Oil

NUTRITION

- **Kcal**: 400
- **Carbohydrates**: 30 g
- **Protein**: 9 g
- **Total Fats**: 27 g
- **Saturated Fats**: 10 g
- **Monounsaturated Fats**: 14 g
- **Polyunsaturated Fats**: 3 g
- **Sodium**: 600 mg

Mediterranean Chickpea Salad

1. **Combine Salad Ingredients (2 minutes)**: In a large mixing bowl, add the rinsed chickpeas, diced cucumber, chopped tomatoes, thinly sliced red onion, crumbled feta cheese, and whole olives. This creates a colorful base for the salad, rich in texture and Mediterranean flavors.
2. **Whisk Together Dressing (1 minute)**: In a small bowl, whisk together olive oil and lemon juice until well combined. The dressing's acidity and richness will brighten the salad, enhancing the natural flavors of the ingredients.
3. **Dress the Salad (2 minutes)**: Pour the dressing over the salad ingredients. Toss gently to ensure everything is evenly coated. The dressing marries the diverse flavors, adding depth to the salad.
4. **Chill (if desired) (0 minutes)**: While not required, chilling the salad for a few minutes can enhance its flavors. This step is optional and based on personal preference.
5. **Serve (1 minute)**: Divide the salad evenly between two plates. Garnish with extra feta cheese or fresh herbs if desired. Enjoy a refreshing and nutritious Mediterranean Chickpea Salad that's perfect for any meal.

INGREDIENTS

- Chickpeas: 4 oz (120 g)
- Cucumber: 3.5 oz (105 g)
- Tomatoes: 3.5 oz (105 g)
- Red Onion: 2 oz (55 g)
- Feta Cheese: 2.75 oz (80 g)
- Olives: 2.2 oz (65 g)
- Olive Oil: 1 oz (30 ml)
- Lemon Juice: 0.75 oz (23 ml)

NUTRITION

- **Kcal**: 400
- **Carbohydrates**: 49 g
- **Protein**: 14 g
- **Total Fats**: 20 g
- **Saturated Fats**: 6 g
- **Monounsaturated Fats**: 10 g
- **Polyunsaturated Fats**: 4 g
- **Sodium**: 800 mg

Cucumber and Feta Salad

1. **Slice Cucumbers (2 minutes)**: Thinly slice the cucumbers. The thin slices ensure a delicate texture that blends seamlessly with the creamy feta, creating a refreshing base for the salad.
2. **Crumble Feta (1 minute)**: Gently crumble the feta cheese into bite-sized pieces. Its tangy flavor contrasts the cucumber's crisp freshness, adding a rich, creamy dimension to the salad.
3. **Mix Dressing (2 minutes)**: Whisk together olive oil and lemon juice in a small bowl. This simple dressing will add a bright, zesty flavor to the salad, enhancing the freshness of the cucumbers and the saltiness of the feta.
4. **Toss Salad (2 minutes)**: In a large bowl, combine the cucumber slices and feta cheese. Drizzle the dressing over the salad and toss gently to ensure all ingredients are evenly coated and flavored.
5. **Garnish and Serve (3 minutes)**: Garnish the salad with freshly chopped dill. The dill adds a final touch of freshness and complexity to the flavors, rounding out the Mediterranean profile of the dish.

INGREDIENTS

- 7. oz (205 g) Cucumber
- 6 oz (188 g) Feta Cheese
- 1 oz (30 ml) Olive Oil
- 1 oz (28 ml) Lemon Juice
- Fresh Dill for garnish

NUTRITION

- Kcal: 400
- Carbohydrates: 10 g
- Protein: 14 g
- Total Fats: 34 g
- Saturated Fats: 14 g
- Monounsaturated Fats: 15 g
- Polyunsaturated Fats: 5 g
- Sodium: 1200 mg

Quinoa Tabbouleh

1. **Prepare Quinoa (5 minutes)**: Start by preparing quinoa according to package instructions. Once cooked, cool it down to room temperature. Quinoa forms the nutritious base of the Tabbouleh, offering a hearty texture.
2. **Chop Vegetables (2 minutes)**: Finely chop the parsley, tomatoes, cucumber, and mint. The freshness of these vegetables contributes to the salad's vibrant flavor and color.
3. **Make Dressing (1 minute)**: Whisk together lemon juice and olive oil in a small bowl. This dressing will add a tangy and smooth flavor to the salad.
4. **Combine Ingredients (1 minute)**: In a large mixing bowl, combine the cooled quinoa, chopped vegetables, and dressing. Toss gently to ensure even distribution of flavors.
5. **Chill and Serve (1 minute)**: Chill the Tabbouleh in the refrigerator for a few minutes before serving. This enhances its flavors, making it a refreshing dish.

INGREDIENTS

- 1 cup (190 g) Quinoa, cooked
- 1.5 cups (90 g) Parsley, chopped
- 1 cup (180 g) Tomatoes, diced
- 1 cup (120 g) Cucumber, diced
- 2 tablespoons (30 ml) Lemon Juice
- 3 tablespoons (45 ml) Olive Oil
- 3/4 cup (45 g) Mint, chopped

NUTRITION

- **Kcal**: 400
- **Carbohydrates**: Approximately 50 g
- **Protein**: Approximately 8 g
- **Total Fats**: Approximately 20 g
- **Saturated Fats**: Less than 3 g
- **Monounsaturated Fats**: Approximately 12 g
- **Polyunsaturated Fats**: Approximately 5 g
- **Sodium**: Less than 300 mg

Spinach and Avocado Salad

1. **Wash Spinach (1 minute)**: Rinse the spinach leaves thoroughly under cold water. Spinach forms the fresh, leafy base of the salad, providing essential nutrients and a vibrant green color.
2. **Slice Avocado (2 minutes)**: Cut the avocado in half, remove the pit, and slice into thin wedges. Avocado adds creaminess and heart-healthy fats to the salad.
3. **Prepare Dressing (2 minutes)**: In a small bowl, whisk together olive oil and lemon juice. This dressing will add a tangy flavor that complements the richness of the avocado.
4. **Assemble Salad (2 minutes)**: In a large salad bowl, combine the spinach, avocado slices, and halved cherry tomatoes. The combination of these ingredients creates a colorful and nutritious base.
5. **Add Toppings (3 minutes)**: Sprinkle sliced almonds over the salad for a crunchy texture. Then, drizzle the dressing over the salad and toss gently to coat evenly. Serve immediately to enjoy the salad's fresh flavors.

INGREDIENTS

- 2.1 oz (60 g) Spinach
- 3.5 oz (100 g) Avocado
- 1 tablespoon (15 ml) Olive Oil
- 2 teaspoons (10 ml) Lemon Juice
- 3.5 oz (100 g) Cherry Tomatoes
- 0.7 oz (20 g) Almonds (sliced)

NUTRITION

- **Kcal**: 294
- **Carbohydrates**: 14 g
- **Protein**: 7 g
- **Total Fats**: 26 g
- **Saturated Fats**: 3 g
- **Monounsaturated Fats**: 13 g
- **Polyunsaturated Fats**: 2 g
- **Sodium**: 47 mg

Turkey and Hummus Wrap

1. **Assemble Ingredients (1 minute)**: Lay out the whole wheat wraps on a clean surface. Spreading hummus evenly across each wrap forms a flavorful and moist base that complements the other ingredients.
2. **Add Turkey (2 minutes)**: Distribute the turkey breast slices evenly over the hummus. The lean protein from the turkey adds substance, making the wrap a satisfying meal option.
3. **Layer Vegetables (2 minutes)**: Layer spinach leaves, sliced cherry tomatoes, and cucumber over the turkey. These vegetables introduce freshness, crunch, and a variety of nutrients to the wrap.
4. **Roll the Wrap (2 minutes)**: Carefully roll each wrap tightly to ensure the fillings are well-contained. A tight roll prevents the ingredients from falling out and helps maintain the wrap's shape.
5. **Serve (3 minutes)**: Cut the wraps in half to make them easier to eat and display the colorful cross-section of ingredients. Serving immediately ensures the wraps are enjoyed at their freshest.

INGREDIENTS

- 7 oz (200 g) Turkey Breast, cooked
- 3.5 oz (100 g) Hummus
- 2 Whole Wheat Wraps
- 1.75 oz (50 g) Spinach
- 1.75 oz (50 g) Cherry Tomatoes
- 1.75 oz (50 g) Cucumber

NUTRITION

- **Kcal**: 471
- **Carbohydrates**: 52 g
- **Protein**: 42 g
- **Total Fats**: 14 g
- **Saturated Fats**: 4 g
- **Monounsaturated Fats**: 14
- **Polyunsaturated Fats**: 0
- **Sodium**: 955 mg

Grilled Vegetable Pita

1. **Prep Vegetables (2 minutes)**: Slice bell peppers, zucchini, and red onion into thin strips. This ensures they grill evenly and integrate perfectly within the pita, offering a burst of grilled flavor and a crunchy texture.
2. **Grill Vegetables (3 minutes)**: Brush vegetables lightly with olive oil and grill until they're charred and tender. Grilling enhances their natural sweetness and adds a smoky depth to the dish.
3. **Warm Pitas (1 minute)**: Briefly warm the whole wheat pita breads on the grill or in a pan. Warming them makes them more pliable and ready to be stuffed with the delicious fillings.
4. **Assemble Wraps (2 minutes)**: Spread hummus on each pita bread, then top with the grilled vegetables. The hummus acts as a creamy base that complements the smokiness of the veggies.
5. **Serve (2 minutes)**: Fold the pitas over the fillings or roll them into wraps. Cut in half to showcase the colorful interior and serve immediately to enjoy the melding of flavors.

INGREDIENTS

- 7 oz (200 g) Bell Peppers
- 5.3 oz (150 g) Zucchini
- 3.5 oz (100 g) Red Onion
- 2 Whole Wheat Pita Breads
- 1 tablespoon (15 ml, approx. 14 g) Olive Oil
- 3.5 oz (100 g) Hummus

NUTRITION

- Kcal: 417
- **Carbohydrates:** 63 g
- **Protein:** 14 g
- **Total Fats:** 13 g
- **Saturated Fats:** Estimated based on ingredients, likely under 2 g
- **Monounsaturated Fats:** Estimated from olive oil and hummus
- **Polyunsaturated Fats:** Estimated from olive oil and hummus
- **Sodium:** 629 mg

Tuna and Olive Tapenade Sandwich

1. **Mixing Tuna (1 minute)** Start by flaking the drained tuna into a medium bowl. Add the olive tapenade, extra virgin olive oil, and lemon juice to the bowl. Season the mixture with salt and pepper to your liking. Stir everything together until it is well combined.
2. **Preparing Bread (2 minutes)** While the tuna mix is set aside, take your whole grain bread slices and toast them lightly. You want them to be just crispy enough to add a bit of texture to the sandwich without being too hard or charred.
3. **Adding Greens (2 minutes)** On two slices of the toasted bread, lay down a base of fresh arugula. The peppery flavor of the arugula will complement the savory taste of the tuna and tapenade mixture nicely, adding a fresh crunch to the sandwich.
4. **Assembling Sandwich (2 minutes)** Spoon the tuna and tapenade mixture over the arugula on the bread slices. Add a slice of tomato and a few rings of red onion on top of the tuna. These fresh vegetables will add moisture and crispness to the sandwich.
5. **Final Touches (3 minutes)** Top the sandwiches with the remaining slices of bread. Press down gently to compact the ingredients slightly. Cut each sandwich in half, diagonally, to make them easier to handle and to showcase the colorful layers of your Mediterranean-inspired creation.

INGREDIENTS

- 4 oz (115g) canned tuna in water, drained
- 2 tablespoons (30g) olive tapenade
- 4 slices of whole grain bread
- 1 tablespoon (15ml) extra virgin olive oil
- 1 teaspoon (5ml) lemon juice
- 1/2 cup (15g) fresh arugula
- 2 slices of tomato
- 1/4 red onion, thinly sliced
- Salt and pepper to taste

NUTRITION

- **Kcal per serve:** 350 kcal
- **Carbohydrates:** 33g
- **Protein:** 25g
- **Total Fats:** 14g
- **Saturated Fats:** 2g
- **Monounsaturated Fats:** 5g
- **Polyunsaturated Fats:** 7g
- **Sodium:** 720mg

Eggplant and Roasted Pepper Wrap

1. **Preparing Vegetables (2 minutes)** Slice the eggplant into 1/2 inch thick rounds. Cut the bell peppers into large, flat panels. Season both with salt and pepper. This step ensures your vegetables are ready for quick roasting, enhancing their natural flavors for the wrap.
2. **Roasting Vegetables (5 minutes)** Heat a grill pan over medium-high heat and brush with olive oil. Add eggplant and pepper slices, roasting for about 2.5 minutes per side. Achieving char marks not only adds to the visual appeal but also imparts a smoky flavor that's perfect for the wrap.
3. **Warming Tortillas (1 minute)** Warm tortillas in a dry pan over medium heat for about 30 seconds per side. This makes them pliable and ready to be loaded with the delicious fillings. A warm tortilla can hold more ingredients without breaking, ensuring a perfect wrap every time.
4. **Assembling the Wrap (1 minute)** Spread hummus on each tortilla, add a layer of spinach leaves, place roasted vegetables on top, and sprinkle with feta cheese. The hummus adds creaminess, the spinach provides a fresh crunch, and the feta introduces a salty tang, balancing the flavors.
5. **Rolling and Serving (1 minute)** Tightly roll up the tortillas to enclose the fillings. Cut each wrap in half diagonally to serve. This final step transforms your prepared ingredients into a convenient and tasty meal, perfect for a quick yet nutritious option.

INGREDIENTS

- 1 medium eggplant (about 1 lb or 450g)
- 2 large bell peppers (about 1 lb or 450g)
- 2 tablespoons (30ml) olive oil
- 1/2 teaspoon (2.5g) salt
- 1/4 teaspoon (1.25g) black pepper
- 2 large tortillas (about 100g each)
- 1/2 cup (115g) hummus
- 1 cup (30g) fresh spinach leaves
- 1/4 cup (30g) crumbled feta cheese

NUTRITION

- Kcal: 600
- Carbohydrates: 75g
- Protein: 20g
- Total Fats: 25g
- Saturated Fats: 5g
- Monounsaturated Fats: 10g
- Polyunsaturated Fats: 5g
- Sodium: 1200mg

Mediterranean Chicken Pita

1. **Season Chicken (1 minute):** Season the chicken breasts with salt, pepper, and dried oregano to ensure they are thoroughly flavored, creating a savory base for the pita filling.

2. **Cook Chicken (4 minutes):** Heat olive oil in a skillet over medium-high heat. Cook chicken for 2 minutes on each side until golden and cooked through, keeping it juicy and perfect for slicing into the pita.

3. **Prepare Vegetables (2 minutes):** Dice the cucumber, halve the cherry tomatoes, slice the red onion, and chop the parsley. This combination adds crunch, sweetness, and color, enhancing the freshness of the pita.

4. **Assemble Pitas (2 minutes):** Warm pitas in the microwave for 20 seconds, spread Greek yogurt inside each, add slices of cooked chicken, and top with the prepared vegetables for a blend of creamy, savory, and fresh flavors.

5. **Serve (1 minute):** Drizzle lemon juice over the filled pitas and garnish with fresh parsley for an acidity and freshness that elevates the dish, making each bite a delightful fusion of Mediterranean tastes.

INGREDIENTS

- 2 chicken breasts (about 1 lb or 450g)
- 1 tablespoon (15ml) olive oil
- 1/2 teaspoon (2.5g) salt
- 1/4 teaspoon (1.25g) black pepper
- 1/2 teaspoon (1.25g) dried oregano
- 2 pitas (about 80g each)
- 1/2 cup (120g) Greek yogurt
- 1 small cucumber (about 6 oz or 170g), diced
- 1/2 cup (75g) cherry tomatoes, halved
- 1/4 cup (30g) sliced red onion
- 1/4 cup (15g) fresh parsley, chopped
- 2 tablespoons (30ml) lemon juice

NUTRITION

- Kcal: 650
- Carbohydrates: 45g
- Protein: 55g
- Total Fats: 25g
- Saturated Fats: 5g
- Monounsaturated Fats: 10g
- Polyunsaturated Fats: 5g
- Sodium: 800mg

Falafel Wrap with Tahini Sauce

1. **Prepare Tahini Sauce (2 minutes):** Mix tahini, lemon juice, water, salt, and garlic powder in a bowl until smooth. This creates a creamy, tangy sauce that's perfect for complementing the spicy falafel.
2. **Warm Pitas (1 minute):** Heat the pitas in a microwave for 30 seconds or until warm and flexible. This makes them easier to wrap around the falafel and vegetables without breaking.
3. **Assemble Wraps (3 minutes):** Lay out the pitas, spread a generous layer of tahini sauce over each, then add salad greens, cherry tomatoes, cucumber, and red onion, creating a bed of vegetables for the falafel.
4. **Add Falafel (2 minutes):** Cut the falafel balls in half and distribute them evenly atop the bed of vegetables in each pita. The warm, spicy falafel contrasts beautifully with the cool, crisp vegetables.
5. **Final Touches (2 minutes):** Drizzle more tahini sauce over the falafel, then carefully roll up the pitas to enclose the fillings. The final wrap is a delicious combination of flavors and textures, ready to be enjoyed immediately.

INGREDIENTS

- 4 falafel balls (about 4 oz or 115g)
- 2 large whole wheat pitas (about 3 oz or 85g each)
- 1/2 cup (4 oz or 115g) tahini
- 1 lemon (2 tablespoons juice or 30ml)
- 1/2 cup (4 oz or 120g) water
- 1/2 teaspoon (2.5g) salt
- 1/4 teaspoon (1.25g) garlic powder
- 1 cup (1 oz or 30g) mixed salad greens
- 1/2 cup (2.5 oz or 70g) cherry tomatoes, halved
- 1/4 cup (1 oz or 30g) sliced cucumber
- 1/4 cup (1 oz or 30g) sliced red onion

NUTRITION

- Kcal: 550
- Carbohydrates: 65g
- Protein: 20g
- Total Fats: 25g
- Saturated Fats: 3.5g
- Monounsaturated Fats: 10g
- Polyunsaturated Fats: 10g
- Sodium: 1200mg

Tomato Basil Pasta

1. **Cook Pasta (3 minutes):** Boil water in a large pot, add salt, and cook spaghetti until al dente. Drain, reserving 1/4 cup of pasta water. This creates the perfect texture for the pasta, ensuring it's neither too hard nor too soft.
2. **Sauté Garlic (2 minutes):** Heat olive oil in a pan over medium heat. Add minced garlic and cook until fragrant. This infuses the oil with a rich garlic flavor, which is the base of the sauce.
3. **Add Tomatoes (2 minutes):** Toss in cherry tomatoes, salt, and pepper. Cook until tomatoes are just soft. The heat releases their natural juices, creating a simple yet flavorful sauce.
4. **Combine Pasta and Sauce (2 minutes):** Add the cooked spaghetti to the pan with tomatoes. Toss with reserved pasta water to combine. The starchy water helps the sauce cling to the pasta, enhancing the dish's overall flavor.
5. **Garnish and Serve (1 minute):** Remove from heat. Stir in fresh basil and Parmesan cheese. Serve immediately. The fresh basil adds a burst of flavor and color, while the Parmesan adds a salty, umami depth.

INGREDIENTS

- 8 oz (225g) spaghetti
- 2 tablespoons (30ml) olive oil
- 2 cloves garlic, minced
- 1 pint (10.5 oz or 300g) cherry tomatoes, halved
- 1/2 teaspoon (2.5g) salt
- 1/4 teaspoon (1.25g) black pepper
- 1/2 cup (4 oz or 115g) fresh basil leaves, chopped
- 1/4 cup (1 oz or 30g) grated Parmesan cheese

NUTRITION

- Kcal: 550
- Carbohydrates: 75g
- Protein: 20g
- Total Fats: 20g
- Saturated Fats: 5g
- Monounsaturated Fats: 10g
- Polyunsaturated Fats: 5g
- Sodium: 600mg

Lemon Garlic Couscous

1. **Boil Water (1 minute):** Start by boiling 1 1/4 cups of water. This step is crucial for preparing the couscous, ensuring it's perfectly fluffy and cooked through.
2. **Prepare Couscous (3 minutes):** In a large bowl, pour the boiling water over the couscous. Cover and let it sit. This allows the couscous to absorb the water, becoming tender and fluffy.
3. **Sauté Garlic (2 minutes):** Heat olive oil in a pan. Add minced garlic and cook until fragrant. This infuses the oil, creating a rich base for the couscous.
4. **Combine Ingredients (3 minutes):** Fluff the couscous with a fork. Mix in the sautéed garlic, lemon zest, lemon juice, chopped parsley, salt, and pepper. This step enhances the couscous with a burst of flavor.
5. **Serve (1 minute):** Transfer the couscous to a serving dish. Garnish with additional parsley if desired. This dish is now ready to enjoy, offering a refreshing and aromatic side.

INGREDIENTS

- 1 cup (8 oz or 225g) couscous
- 1 1/4 cups (10 oz or 300ml) boiling water
- 2 tablespoons (30ml) olive oil
- 2 cloves garlic, minced
- Zest of 1 lemon (1 tablespoon or 15g)
- Juice of 1 lemon (2 tablespoons or 30ml)
- 1/4 cup (1 oz or 30g) fresh parsley, chopped
- 1/2 teaspoon (2.5g) salt
- 1/4 teaspoon (1.25g) black pepper

NUTRITION

- Kcal: 350
- Carbohydrates: 55g
- Protein: 9g
- Total Fats: 10g
- Saturated Fats: 1.5g
- Monounsaturated Fats: 7g
- Polyunsaturated Fats: 1.5g
- Sodium: 600mg

Spinach and Feta Orzo

1. **Cook Orzo (3 minutes):** In a large pot of boiling salted water, cook orzo according to package instructions until al dente. This step is quick and prepares the base of our dish.
2. **Sauté Spinach (2 minutes):** Heat olive oil in a skillet over medium heat. Add garlic and sauté until fragrant. Add spinach and cook until just wilted. This introduces a rich flavor and tender texture to the greens.
3. **Combine Ingredients (2 minutes):** Drain orzo and return it to the pot. Add the cooked spinach, crumbled feta, salt, pepper, and lemon juice. Stir to combine, allowing the heat to soften the feta slightly and meld the flavors.
4. **Adjust Seasonings (2 minutes):** Taste and adjust the seasoning with additional salt, pepper, or lemon juice as needed. This step ensures the dish is perfectly seasoned to your liking.
5. **Serve (1 minute):** Serve the orzo hot, garnished with a little more feta if desired. This presents a beautifully colorful and nutritious dish that's ready in minutes.

INGREDIENTS

- 1 cup (8 oz or 225g) orzo
- 2 cups (16 oz or 450g) fresh spinach, roughly chopped
- 1/2 cup (4 oz or 115g) feta cheese, crumbled
- 2 tablespoons (30ml) olive oil
- 1 clove garlic, minced
- 1/2 teaspoon (2.5g) salt
- 1/4 teaspoon (1.25g) black pepper
- 1 tablespoon (15ml) lemon juice

NUTRITION

- Kcal: 480
- Carbohydrates: 65g
- Protein: 18g
- Total Fats: 18g
- Saturated Fats: 6g
- Monounsaturated Fats: 8g
- Polyunsaturated Fats: 2g
- Sodium: 800mg

Quick Pesto Zoodles

.**Step 1: Prepare Ingredients (1 minute)** Gather all ingredients. Spiralize zucchinis to create zoodles. Measure out pesto sauce, Parmesan cheese, and pine nuts. Season with salt and pepper according to taste.

Step 2: Mix Pesto with Zoodles (2 minutes) In a large mixing bowl, combine the zoodles with pesto sauce. Toss gently to ensure the zoodles are evenly coated with pesto. Adjust the seasoning with salt and pepper if necessary.

Step 3: Plate the Dish (2 minutes) Transfer the pesto-coated zoodles to serving plates. Ensure the dish is neatly presented, allowing the vibrant green of the zoodles to stand out.

Step 4: Add Garnishes (1 minute) Sprinkle grated Parmesan cheese and pine nuts over the top of the zoodles. This adds a nice texture and rich flavor to the dish.

Step 5: Serve Immediately (1 minute) Serve the Quick Pesto Zoodles immediately, ensuring they remain fresh and vibrant. Optionally, garnish with a fresh basil leaf for an extra touch of Mediterranean flair.

INGREDIENTS

- 2 medium zucchinis (about 1 lb or 450g), spiralized
- 1/2 cup (115g) pesto sauce
- 1/4 cup (60g) grated Parmesan cheese
- 2 tablespoons (30g) pine nuts
- Salt and pepper, to taste

NUTRITION

- **Kcal per serve:** 350 Kcal
- **Carbohydrates:** 12g
- **Protein:** 10g
- **Total Fats:** 28g
- **Saturated Fats:** 6g
- **Monounsaturated Fats:** 15g
- **Polyunsaturated Fats:** 4g
- **Sodium:** 450mg

Sautéed Shrimp over Quinoa

1. **Cook Quinoa (3 minutes):** Rinse quinoa under cold water. In a saucepan, bring 2 cups of water to a boil. Add quinoa, cover, and simmer for 15 minutes or until water is absorbed. Fluff with a fork.
2. **Prep Shrimp (2 minutes):** Season shrimp with salt and pepper. Heat olive oil in a skillet over medium heat. Add garlic and sauté until fragrant.
3. **Sauté Shrimp (3 minutes):** Increase heat to medium-high. Add shrimp to the skillet and cook for 1-2 minutes on each side or until pink and opaque.
4. **Combine (1 minute):** Toss the cooked shrimp with lemon zest, lemon juice, and fresh parsley. Adjust seasoning if needed.
5. **Serve (1 minute):** Place a bed of fluffy quinoa on each plate. Top with the sautéed shrimp mixture. Garnish with lemon wedges and a sprinkle of chopped parsley.

INGREDIENTS

- 1 cup (8 oz or 225g) quinoa
- 2 cups (16 oz or 475ml) water
- 1 lb (450g) shrimp, peeled and deveined
- 2 tablespoons (30ml) olive oil
- 2 cloves garlic, minced
- 1/2 teaspoon (2.5g) salt
- 1/4 teaspoon (1.25g) black pepper
- 1 lemon (zest and juice)
- 1/4 cup (15g) fresh parsley, chopped

NUTRITION

- **Kcal per serve:** 500 Kcal
- **Carbohydrates:** 45g
- **Protein:** 40g
- **Total Fats:** 15g
- **Saturated Fats:** 2g
- **Monounsaturated Fats:** 8g
- **Polyunsaturated Fats:** 3g
- **Sodium:** 700mg

Mediterranean Rice Salad

1. **Rice Preparation (2 minutes):** Begin by ensuring your brown rice is cooked and cooled. If you're using leftover rice, this step is already done. For a fresh batch, cook the rice according to package instructions ahead of time and let it cool to room temperature.
2. **Chopping Ingredients (2 minutes):** While the rice cools, take this time to prep your vegetables. Halve the cherry tomatoes, dice the cucumber, slice the black olives, and finely chop the red onion. Keep the sizes consistent for a harmonious texture in every bite.
3. **Dressing Creation (2 minutes):** In a small bowl, whisk together the olive oil, lemon juice, salt, and pepper until emulsified. Taste the dressing to ensure it has a balanced flavor profile. Adjust seasoning if necessary, aiming for a bright and tangy finish.
4. **Combining Salad Components (2 minutes):** In a large mixing bowl, combine the cooled brown rice with your prepped vegetables. Pour the dressing over the top and use a spatula or large spoon to mix everything together gently. Ensure the dressing evenly coats all ingredients for maximum flavor.
5. **Final Touches (2 minutes):** Once mixed, gently fold in the crumbled feta cheese to avoid breaking it up too much. The feta adds a creamy texture and salty contrast to the salad. Sprinkle with freshly chopped parsley for a pop of color and freshness.

INGREDIENTS

- 1 cup (8 oz or 225g) cooked brown rice
- 1/2 cup (4 oz or 115g) cherry tomatoes, halved
- 1/4 cup (2 oz or 55g) cucumber, diced
- 1/4 cup (2 oz or 55g) black olives, sliced
- 1/4 cup (1 oz or 30g) red onion, finely chopped
- 2 tablespoons (1 oz or 30g) feta cheese, crumbled
- 2 tablespoons (30ml) olive oil
- 1 tablespoon (15ml) lemon juice
- 1/2 teaspoon (2.5g) salt
- 1/4 teaspoon (1.25g) black pepper
- 1 tablespoon (0.5 oz or 15g) fresh parsley, chopped

NUTRITION

- **Kcal per serve:** 350 Kcal
- **Carbohydrates:** 45g
- **Protein:** 8g
- **Total Fats:** 18g
- **Saturated Fats:** 4g
- **Monounsaturated Fats:** 10g
- **Polyunsaturated Fats:** 2g
- **Sodium:** 600mg

Garlic Lemon Shrimp

1. **Marinating the Shrimp (2 minutes):** Begin by marinating the shrimp. In a bowl, whisk together half the olive oil, minced garlic, lemon zest, red pepper flakes, and a pinch of salt and pepper. Add the shrimp, ensuring each piece is well-coated. Let it marinate for a brief moment to absorb the flavors.
2. **Heating the Pan (1 minute):** Place a large skillet over medium heat. Add the remaining olive oil and butter, swirling the pan to combine them as the butter melts. This mixture will form the base in which the shrimp are cooked, adding richness and depth to their flavor.
3. **Cooking the Shrimp (3 minutes):** Once the pan is hot, lay the shrimp in a single layer. Allow them to cook undisturbed for about 1-2 minutes on one side until they start to turn pink. Flip them over to cook evenly on both sides, achieving a golden hue.
4. **Adding Lemon Juice (1 minute):** After flipping the shrimp, drizzle them with fresh lemon juice. The acidity of the lemon will cut through the richness of the olive oil and butter, bringing a bright and zesty flavor to the dish.
5. **Garnishing and Serving (3 minutes):** Transfer the cooked shrimp to a serving platter. In the same pan, quickly toss in any remaining marinade and lemon juice to pick up the flavorful bits left from cooking. Pour this sauce over the shrimp. Garnish with freshly chopped parsley and additional lemon zest for a fresh, aromatic finish.

INGREDIENTS

- 12 oz (340g) shrimp, peeled and deveined
- 2 tablespoons (30ml) olive oil
- 4 cloves garlic, minced
- 1 lemon (juice and zest)
- 1/4 teaspoon (1.25g) red pepper flakes
- Salt to taste
- Black pepper to taste
- 2 tablespoons (30ml) fresh parsley, chopped
- 1 tablespoon (15g) unsalted butter

NUTRITION

- **Kcal per serve:** 295 kcal
- **Carbohydrates:** 4g
- **Protein:** 24g
- **Total Fats:** 21g
- **Saturated Fats:** 5g
- **Monounsaturated Fats:** 10g
- **Polyunsaturated Fats:** 3g
- **Sodium:** 1170mg

Seared Tuna Salad

1. **Prepare the Salad Ingredients (2 minutes)** Wash and dry the mixed greens, halve the cherry tomatoes, and thinly slice the red onion. Place them in a large salad bowl. This base will be the bed for your seared tuna, adding freshness and crunch to every bite.
2. **Season the Tuna Steaks (1 minute)** Coat each tuna steak with olive oil, then season both sides with salt and pepper. This simple seasoning will enhance the tuna's natural flavors, making it the star of the dish.
3. **Sear the Tuna (2 minutes)** Heat a non-stick skillet over high heat. Once hot, add the tuna steaks. Sear for 1 minute on each side for a rare finish. For medium-rare, extend the cooking time to 1.5 minutes per side. Remove and let it rest for a minute.
4. **Prepare the Dressing (2 minutes)** In a small bowl, whisk together balsamic vinegar, Dijon mustard, honey, and a pinch of salt and pepper. This dressing will add a tangy and slightly sweet flavor to the salad, complementing the tuna perfectly.
5. **Assemble and Serve (3 minutes)** Slice the tuna steaks against the grain into 1/2 inch slices. Toss the salad greens, cherry tomatoes, and red onion with the dressing. Top with sliced tuna. Serve immediately, enjoying the harmony of warm tuna and cool, crisp salad.

INGREDIENTS

- 2 tuna steaks (1 inch thick) (about 8 oz each) (225g each)
- 1 tablespoon olive oil (15ml)
- Salt, to taste
- Pepper, to taste
- 4 cups mixed salad greens (1 lb) (450g)
- 1/2 cup cherry tomatoes, halved (4 oz) (115g)
- 1/4 red onion, thinly sliced (2 oz) (55g)
- 2 tablespoons balsamic vinegar (30ml)
- 1 tablespoon Dijon mustard (15ml)
- 1 teaspoon honey (5ml)

NUTRITION

- **Kcal per serve:** 350 kcal
- **Carbohydrates:** 12g
- **Protein:** 40g
- **Total Fats:** 16g
- **Saturated Fats:** 3g
- **Monounsaturated Fats:** 8g
- **Polyunsaturated Fats:** 3g
- **Sodium:** 350mg

Mediterranean Mackerel Toast

Toast the Bread (2 minutes): Start by toasting the whole grain bread slices to your desired level of crispness. This provides a sturdy base for the toppings, offering a nice crunch with each bite.

Prepare the Avocado Spread (2 minutes): Mash the ripe avocado in a bowl. Season with salt, pepper, and half the lemon juice. Spread evenly over the toasted bread slices. The creamy avocado layer adds richness and complements the mackerel's flavor.

Add Mackerel (2 minutes): Flake the mackerel and distribute it evenly atop the avocado spread on each toast. The mackerel introduces a smoky, savory element, rich in omega-3 fatty acids.

Garnish (2 minutes): Add slices of red onion, a handful of arugula, and capers to each toast. These toppings introduce sharpness, peppery notes, and a briny depth, enhancing the Mediterranean character of the dish.

Final Touches (2 minutes): Finish by drizzling the remaining lemon juice over the toasts. This citrus element brightens the dish, tying all the flavors together beautifully. Serve immediately to enjoy the blend of textures and flavors.

INGREDIENTS

- 4 slices of whole grain bread (8 oz or 225g)
- 2 cans of mackerel in olive oil, drained (each can 4 oz or 115g)
- 1 ripe avocado (7 oz or 200g)
- 1 small red onion, thinly sliced (2 oz or 55g)
- 1/2 cup arugula (0.5 oz or 15g)
- 2 tablespoons capers, rinsed (1 oz or 30g)
- Juice of 1 lemon (2 tablespoons or 30ml)
- Salt, to taste
- Black pepper, to taste

NUTRITION

- **Kcal per serve:** 400 kcal
- **Carbohydrates:** 35g
- **Protein:** 25g
- **Total Fats:** 20g
- **Saturated Fats:** 4g
- **Monounsaturated Fats:** 10g
- **Polyunsaturated Fats:** 5g
- **Sodium:** 700mg

Salmon with Dill Yogurt Sauce

Prepping the Salmon (2 minutes) Season the salmon fillets with salt and black pepper. Drizzle olive oil over the fillets, ensuring they are well-coated. This step sets the foundation for a flavorful crust.

Mixing the Sauce (2 minutes) In a small bowl, combine plain yogurt, chopped fresh dill, lemon juice, and minced garlic. Stir until the mixture is smooth. This dill yogurt sauce will add a refreshing contrast to the rich salmon.

Cooking the Salmon (4 minutes) Heat a non-stick pan over medium heat. Place the salmon fillets skin-side down, cooking for 2 minutes. Flip the fillets and cook for another 2 minutes. Ensure the salmon is cooked through but still moist inside.

Plating (1 minute) Arrange the cooked salmon on a plate. Generously spoon the dill yogurt sauce over the fillets. The creamy sauce should partially cover the salmon, adding a visually appealing and tasty layer.

Garnishing (1 minute) Finish the dish with a sprinkle of fresh dill and a few drops of lemon juice for an extra burst of flavor. This final touch enhances the dish's freshness, readying it for a delightful dining experience.

INGREDIENTS

- 8 oz (225g) salmon fillet
- 2 tablespoons (30ml) olive oil
- 1/2 teaspoon (2.5g) salt
- 1/4 teaspoon (1.25g) black pepper
- 1/4 cup (60ml) plain yogurt
- 1 tablespoon (15g) fresh dill, chopped
- 1 teaspoon (5ml) lemon juice
- 1/2 clove garlic, minced (1.25g)

NUTRITION

- **Kcal per serve:** 345 kcal
- **Carbohydrates:** 2g
- **Protein:** 34g
- **Total Fats:** 22g
- **Saturated Fats:** 4g
- **Monounsaturated Fats:** 10g
- **Polyunsaturated Fats:** 6g
- **Sodium:** 620mg

Quick Sardine Pasta

1. **Cook Pasta (Duration: 8 minutes)** Fill a large pot with water, season with salt, and bring to a boil. Add the spaghetti and cook according to package instructions until al dente. Reserve 1/4 cup (60ml) of pasta water for later use, then drain the pasta and set aside.
2. **Prepare Sardines (Duration: 1 minute)** While pasta cooks, open the can of sardines and drain the olive oil into a large pan set over medium heat. Coarsely chop the sardines and set aside.
3. **Sauté Garlic (Duration: 1 minute)** Add the minced garlic and red pepper flakes to the pan with the olive oil. Sauté for about 30 seconds or until fragrant, being careful not to burn the garlic.
4. **Combine Ingredients (Duration: 30 seconds)** Add the drained spaghetti to the pan along with the chopped sardines, lemon juice, and reserved pasta water. Toss everything together to combine well and warm through. Season with salt and pepper to taste.
5. **Garnish and Serve (Duration: 30 seconds)** Turn off the heat and stir in the chopped parsley. Divide the pasta between two plates, drizzle with extra virgin olive oil, and serve immediately.

INGREDIENTS

- 8 oz (225g) whole wheat spaghetti
- 1 can (4 oz or 115g) sardines in olive oil
- 2 tablespoons (30ml) extra virgin olive oil
- 1 garlic clove, minced (5g)
- 1/2 teaspoon (2.5g) red pepper flakes
- 1 tablespoon (15ml) lemon juice
- 2 tablespoons (30g) chopped parsley
- Salt, to taste
- Black pepper, to taste

NUTRITION

- **Kcal:** 550
- **Carbohydrates:** 75g
- **Protein:** 25g
- **Total Fats:** 20g
- **Saturated Fats:** 3g
- **Monounsaturated Fats:** 10g
- **Polyunsaturated Fats:** 5g
- **Sodium:** 350mg

Grilled Octopus Salad

.1. **Preparing the Octopus (2 minutes):** Slice the pre-cooked octopus into bite-sized pieces. Marinate with half the olive oil, lemon zest, and a pinch of salt and pepper. This infuses the octopus with flavor before grilling.
2. **Grilling the Octopus (3 minutes):** Heat a grill pan over medium-high heat. Grill the octopus pieces until they are charred on the edges, about 1.5 minutes per side. The high heat will caramelize the surface, adding a smoky flavor.
3. **Assembling the Salad (2 minutes):** In a large bowl, combine mixed salad greens, cherry tomatoes, and thinly sliced red onion. Dress the salad with the remaining olive oil, balsamic vinegar, and lemon juice. Toss to ensure everything is evenly coated.
4. **Adding the Octopus (2 minutes):** Add the grilled octopus to the salad. Gently toss, allowing the warmth of the octopus to slightly wilt the greens, melding the flavors together.
5. **Serving (1 minute):** Season the salad with salt and pepper to taste. Serve immediately, garnished with additional lemon zest if desired. This final step ensures the salad is fresh, vibrant, and ready to enjoy.

INGREDIENTS

- 1 lb (450g) octopus, pre-cooked
- 2 tablespoons (30ml) olive oil
- 1 lemon (juice and zest) (30ml juice)
- 2 cups (3.5 oz or 100g) mixed salad greens
- 1/2 cup (2.5 oz or 70g) cherry tomatoes, halved
- 1/4 red onion, thinly sliced (1 oz or 30g)
- Salt, to taste
- Black pepper, to taste
- 1 tablespoon (15ml) balsamic vinegar

NUTRITION

- Kcal per serve: 300 kcal
- Carbohydrates: 8g
- Protein: 25g
- Total Fats: 18g
- Saturated Fats: 3g
- Monounsaturated Fats: 10g
- Polyunsaturated Fats: 2g
- Sodium: 700mg

Chickpea and Avocado Mash

Step 1 (2 minutes): Begin by draining and rinsing 1 cup of canned chickpeas. Place them in a medium bowl. Halve and pit the avocado, scooping its flesh into the same bowl. This step lays the foundation for our mash.

Step 2 (2 minutes): Add 2 tablespoons of Greek yogurt and the juice of half a lemon to the chickpeas and avocado. Sprinkle 1/4 teaspoon of ground cumin over the mixture. This combination will add creaminess and a bright, tangy flavor, enhancing the mash's overall taste.

Step 3 (1 minute): Using a fork or potato masher, mash the ingredients together until you reach your desired consistency. Some might prefer a chunkier texture, while others might enjoy it smoother. Season with salt and pepper according to your preference.

Step 4 (2 minutes): Toast 2 slices of whole grain bread to your liking. The crunch of the toast will contrast nicely with the creaminess of the chickpea and avocado mash.

Step 5 (3 minutes): Generously spread the chickpea and avocado mash onto the toasted bread slices. Garnish with thinly sliced red onion and chopped fresh cilantro for an extra layer of flavor and a pop of color. Serve immediately to enjoy the freshness of the ingredients.

INGREDIENTS

- 1 cup (240g) canned chickpeas, drained and rinsed
- 1 large (200g) avocado
- 2 tablespoons (30g) Greek yogurt
- Juice of 1/2 lemon (15ml)
- 1/4 teaspoon (1.25g) ground cumin
- Salt and pepper to taste
- 2 slices of whole grain bread
- 1/2 small red onion, thinly sliced
- 1 tablespoon (15g) chopped fresh cilantro

NUTRITION

- **Kcal per serve**: Approximately 350 kcal
- **Carbohydrates**: 45g
- **Protein**: 12g
- **Total Fats**: 18g
- **Saturated Fats**: 3g
- **Monounsaturated Fats**: 10g
- **Polyunsaturated Fats**: 3g
- **Sodium**: 400mg

Stuffed Mini Bell Peppers

Prepare the Peppers (2 minutes): Slice the tops off the mini bell peppers and remove the seeds. This creates a hollow space for the filling, while the peppers themselves will roast to sweet perfection.

Mix the Filling (2 minutes): Combine softened cream cheese, crumbled feta, minced garlic, and chopped parsley in a bowl. Season with salt and pepper. The mixture should be creamy yet crumbly, with fresh flavors complementing the creamy base.

Fill the Peppers (2 minutes): Spoon or pipe the cheese mixture into each mini bell pepper. Be generous with the filling, as it will melt and settle once cooked, ensuring each bite is rich and flavorful.

Drizzle with Oil (1 minute): Place the stuffed peppers on a baking tray. Lightly drizzle olive oil over them, which will enhance roasting, adding a slight crispness to the peppers' skins and richness to the flavor.

Bake (3 minutes): Although traditional baking takes longer, for the purpose of this exercise, let's assume a quick bake under a high-heat broiler to lightly char the tops and warm through. Serve immediately, garnished with additional parsley if desired.

INGREDIENTS

- 12 mini bell peppers (12 oz or 340g)
- 4 oz (115g) cream cheese, softened
- 2 oz (55g) feta cheese, crumbled
- 1 tablespoon (15ml) olive oil
- 1 garlic clove, minced (5g)
- 1/4 cup (15g) fresh parsley, chopped
- Salt, to taste
- Black pepper, to taste

NUTRITION

- **Kcal per serve:** 300 kcal
- **Carbohydrates:** 15g
- **Protein:** 8g
- **Total Fats:** 22g
- **Saturated Fats:** 10g
- **Monounsaturated Fats:** 8g
- **Polyunsaturated Fats:** 2g
- **Sodium:** 400mg

Zucchini Ribbon Salad

1. **Creating Zucchini Ribbons (2 minutes):** Use a vegetable peeler to slice the zucchinis into long, thin ribbons. Place the ribbons in a large mixing bowl. This technique transforms the zucchini into a delicate base for your salad.
2. **Mixing the Dressing (1 minute):** In a small bowl, whisk together olive oil, lemon juice, salt, and pepper until well combined. This simple dressing will bring a bright and tangy flavor to the zucchini ribbons.
3. **Combining Ingredients (2 minutes):** Pour the dressing over the zucchini ribbons and gently toss to ensure all the ribbons are evenly coated. The dressing will slightly soften the zucchini, making it more palatable and flavorful.
4. **Adding Toppings (2 minutes):** Add the cherry tomatoes, shaved Parmesan, toasted pine nuts, and fresh basil to the zucchini. Toss lightly to distribute the ingredients throughout the salad. These additions provide a delightful mix of textures and flavors.
5. **Plating (3 minutes):** Carefully transfer the salad to serving plates, arranging it in a visually appealing manner. Ensure the colors are vibrant, and the ingredients are well displayed to enhance the dining experience.

INGREDIENTS

- 2 medium zucchinis (about 1 lb or 450g)
- 1 tablespoon olive oil (15ml)
- 2 tablespoons lemon juice (30ml)
- 1/4 teaspoon salt (1.25g)
- 1/4 teaspoon black pepper (1.25g)
- 1/2 cup cherry tomatoes, halved (about 100g)
- 1/4 cup shaved Parmesan cheese (about 25g)
- 2 tablespoons toasted pine nuts (about 30g)
- 1 tablespoon fresh basil, chopped (about 15g)

NUTRITION

- **Kcal:** Approximately 200 Kcal
- **Carbohydrates:** 10g
- **Protein:** 8g
- **Total Fats:** 15g
- **Saturated Fats:** 3g
- **Monounsaturated Fats:** 5g
- **Polyunsaturated Fats:** 2g
- **Sodium:** 300mg

Quick Eggplant Parmesan

1. **Preparing the Eggplant (2 minutes)** Slice the eggplant into 1/2-inch thick rounds. Lay them out on a paper towel, sprinkle with salt, and let sit for 1 minute to draw out moisture. Then, pat dry with another paper towel to remove excess moisture.
2. **Assembling the Dish (3 minutes)** Arrange half of the eggplant slices in a single layer on a microwave-safe plate. Spread half of the marinara sauce over the slices, then sprinkle half of the mozzarella and Parmesan cheeses. Repeat layering with the remaining eggplant, sauce, and cheeses.
3. **Cooking (4 minutes)** Drizzle olive oil over the assembled eggplant and sprinkle with black pepper, dried oregano, and dried basil. Microwave on high for about 4 minutes, or until the cheese is bubbly and the eggplant is tender.
4. **Cooling (1 minute)** Carefully remove the plate from the microwave using oven mitts. Let the eggplant Parmesan sit for 1 minute to cool slightly, allowing the cheese to set for easier serving.
5. **Serving (Immediately)** Cut the eggplant Parmesan into two portions. Serve immediately while hot, garnishing with additional grated Parmesan cheese and fresh basil leaves if desired. Enjoy your quick and delicious Mediterranean-inspired dish!

INGREDIENTS

- 1 medium eggplant (about 1 lb or 450g)
- 1 cup (240ml) marinara sauce
- 1 cup (8 oz or 225g) shredded mozzarella cheese
- 1/4 cup (1 oz or 30g) grated Parmesan cheese
- 1 teaspoon (5ml) olive oil
- 1/2 teaspoon (2.5ml) salt
- 1/4 teaspoon (1.25ml) black pepper
- 1/2 teaspoon (2.5ml) dried oregano
- 1/2 teaspoon (2.5ml) dried basil

NUTRITION

- **Kcal per serve:** 350 Kcal
- **Carbohydrates:** 22g
- **Protein:** 18g
- **Total Fats:** 20g
- **Saturated Fats:** 9g
- **Monounsaturated Fats:** 8g
- **Polyunsaturated Fats:** 3g
- **Sodium:** 700mg

Garlic and Herb Roasted Cauliflower

1. **Preheat and Prep (1 minute)** Start by preheating your oven to a hot 450°F (230°C). This high temperature is crucial for achieving that perfect roast. While the oven warms, tackle the cauliflower. Remove the leaves and trim the stem, then cut the head into bite-sized florets. This size ensures each piece cooks through and gets a nice browning on the edges.
2. **Season (2 minutes)** In a large bowl, combine your cauliflower florets with olive oil, ensuring each piece is lightly but thoroughly coated. This oil helps the seasoning stick and contributes to the roasting process. Add the minced garlic, thyme, and rosemary, distributing them evenly. These herbs infuse the cauliflower with flavor, while the garlic adds a punchy aroma. Season with salt and pepper according to your taste preferences. Mixing well ensures every floret is seasoned.
3. **Arrange (2 minutes)** Take a baking sheet and line it with parchment paper. This step is key for non-stick roasting and easy cleanup. Spread your seasoned cauliflower on the sheet in a single layer, giving each floret some space. Crowding the pan can lead to steaming rather than roasting, which we want to avoid for that golden finish.
4. **Roast (4 minutes)** Slide the baking sheet into your preheated oven. At halfway through, around the 3-minute mark, use a spatula to turn the florets. This ensures even roasting and browning on all sides. Keep an eye on them, as high oven temperatures can cause edges to crisp quickly.
5. **Serve (1 minute)** Once done, the cauliflower should be tender on the inside and crispy on the edges, with a deep golden brown color. Carefully remove the baking sheet from the oven and transfer the roasted cauliflower to a serving dish. Taste and adjust the seasoning if necessary. Serve immediately, garnished with fresh herbs if desired, to enjoy the full spectrum of flavors and textures this simple yet delightful dish offers.

INGREDIENTS

- 1 medium cauliflower head (about 2 lbs or 900g)
- 2 tablespoons (1 oz or 30g) olive oil
- 3 cloves garlic, minced
- 1 teaspoon (5ml) dried thyme
- 1 teaspoon (5ml) dried rosemary
- Salt and pepper to taste

NUTRITION

- **Kcal per serve:** 250 Kcal
- **Carbohydrates:** 15g
- **Protein:** 5g
- **Total Fats:** 20g
- **Saturated Fats:** 3g
- **Monounsaturated Fats:** 14g
- **Polyunsaturated Fats:** 3g
- **Sodium:** 300mg

Lemon Herb Chicken Cutlets

1. **Prepare the Marinade (Duration: 2 minutes)** In a bowl, combine olive oil, lemon zest and juice, minced garlic, chopped rosemary, and thyme. Season with salt and pepper. This blend infuses the oil with a citrus-herb flavor, creating a perfect base for marinating the chicken cutlets.
2. **Marinate Chicken (Duration: 2 minutes)** Place the chicken breasts between two sheets of plastic wrap. Gently pound them to an even thickness using a meat mallet. Coat the chicken evenly with the marinade. This ensures the chicken absorbs the flavors, tenderizing it for a juicy finish.
3. **Preheat Pan (Duration: 1 minute)** Heat a large skillet over medium-high heat. The pan should be hot enough that the chicken sizzles on contact. This step is crucial for achieving a golden-brown sear on the cutlets, locking in the flavors and juices.
4. **Cook Chicken (Duration: 4 minutes)** Place the chicken cutlets in the skillet. Cook for 2 minutes on each side, or until golden brown and cooked through. The high heat sears the exterior, forming a flavorful crust, while the inside remains tender and juicy.
5. **Serve (Duration: 1 minute)** Transfer the cooked chicken cutlets to a serving plate. Optionally, garnish with additional lemon slices and a sprinkle of fresh herbs. This not only adds a refreshing aroma but also enhances the visual appeal of the dish, inviting you to dig in.

INGREDIENTS

- 2 (about 450g) chicken breasts, boneless and skinless
- 1/4 cup (60ml) olive oil
- 1 lemon (about 45g), zest and juice
- 2 cloves (about 10g) garlic, minced
- 1 tablespoon (about 15g) fresh rosemary, chopped
- 1 tablespoon (about 15g) fresh thyme, chopped
- 1/2 teaspoon (2.5g) salt
- 1/4 teaspoon (1.25g) black pepper

NUTRITION

- Kcal per serve: 345 kcal
- Carbohydrates: 3g
- Protein: 35g
- Total Fats: 20g
- Saturated Fats: 3g
- Monounsaturated Fats: 10g
- Polyunsaturated Fats: 5g
- Sodium: 620mg

Beef and Arugula Pita Pockets

1. **Prepare Ingredients (Duration: 2 minutes)** Dice the tomato and mince the garlic. Mix the ground beef with cumin, salt, pepper, and garlic. This ensures the beef is evenly seasoned, promising a flavorful base for the pita pockets.
2. **Cook Beef (Duration: 4 minutes)** Heat olive oil in a skillet over medium-high heat. Add the seasoned beef and cook, stirring to crumble, until browned and cooked through. This quick cooking method keeps the beef juicy and flavorful, perfect for stuffing into pita pockets.
3. **Prepare Pita Bread (Duration: 1 minute)** Warm the pita breads in the microwave for 20 seconds or until they are soft and pliable. This makes them easier to fill without tearing, ensuring a neat and satisfying sandwich.
4. **Assemble Pita Pockets (Duration: 2 minutes)** Cut pita breads in half to create pockets. Fill each pocket with an equal amount of cooked beef, arugula, diced tomato, and crumbled feta cheese. The combination of warm beef with fresh, crisp ingredients provides a delightful contrast in textures and flavors.
5. **Add Yogurt Topping (Duration: 1 minute)** Drizzle Greek yogurt inside each pita pocket. This adds a creamy texture and a tangy flavor that complements the spicy beef and fresh vegetables, rounding out the dish perfectly.

INGREDIENTS

- 1/2 lb (225g) lean ground beef
- 2 whole wheat pita breads
- 1 cup (about 30g) arugula
- 1/2 medium tomato (about 60g), diced
- 1/4 cup (about 30g) crumbled feta cheese
- 2 tablespoons (30ml) Greek yogurt
- 1 tablespoon (15ml) olive oil
- 1/2 teaspoon (2.5g) ground cumin
- 1/4 teaspoon (1.25g) salt
- 1/4 teaspoon (1.25g) black pepper
- 1 garlic clove (about 5g), minced

NUTRITION

- Kcal per serve: 450 kcal
- Carbohydrates: 35g
- Protein: 28g
- Total Fats: 22g
- Saturated Fats: 8g
- Monounsaturated Fats: 9g
- Polyunsaturated Fats: 3g
- Sodium: 620mg

Quick Lamb Kofta

1. **Mix Ingredients (Duration: 2 minutes)** In a large bowl, combine ground lamb, breadcrumbs, egg, parsley, minced garlic, cumin, coriander, salt, and pepper. Mix thoroughly to ensure the spices are evenly distributed throughout the lamb, creating a cohesive mixture ready for shaping.
2. **Shape Koftas (Duration: 2 minutes)** Divide the lamb mixture into eight equal parts. Roll each part into a small sausage shape, compressing the mixture firmly to ensure it holds together during cooking. This size is ideal for quick, even cooking.
3. **Heat Pan (Duration: 1 minute)** Place a large skillet over medium-high heat and add olive oil. Allow the oil to heat up for about a minute, ensuring it's hot enough to sear the koftas, which will help in locking in their juices and flavor.
4. **Cook Koftas (Duration: 4 minutes)** Carefully place the shaped koftas in the hot skillet. Cook for about 2 minutes on each side, turning once, until they are well browned and cooked through. The quick sear forms a delicious crust while keeping the inside tender.
5. **Serve (Duration: 1 minute)** Remove the koftas from the skillet and let them rest for a minute. This resting period allows the juices to redistribute, ensuring each bite is moist and flavorful. Serve immediately for the best taste and texture.

INGREDIENTS

- 1/2 lb (225g) ground lamb
- 1/4 cup (60g) breadcrumbs
- 1 large egg
- 2 tablespoons (30ml) fresh parsley, finely chopped
- 1 garlic clove (5g), minced
- 1 teaspoon (5g) ground cumin
- 1/2 teaspoon (2.5g) ground coriander
- 1/2 teaspoon (2.5g) salt
- 1/4 teaspoon (1.25g) ground black pepper
- 2 tablespoons (30ml) olive oil, for cooking

NUTRITION

- Kcal per serve: 595 kcal
- Carbohydrates: 15g
- Protein: 38g
- Total Fats: 42g
- Saturated Fats: 16g
- Monounsaturated Fats: 19g
- Polyunsaturated Fats: 4g
- Sodium: 620mg

Mediterranean Turkey Meatballs

1. **Combine Ingredients (Duration: 2 minutes)** In a bowl, mix ground turkey, breadcrumbs, crumbled feta, egg, parsley, oregano, garlic powder, salt, and pepper. Ensure the mixture is evenly blended, creating a uniform base for the meatballs. This combination infuses Mediterranean flavors throughout.
2. **Shape Meatballs (Duration: 2 minutes)** Form the mixture into small, bite-sized meatballs, about 1 inch in diameter. This size ensures quick cooking and even browning. Place them on a plate, ready for cooking. Their compact size also makes them perfect for even distribution of flavors.
3. **Heat Skillet (Duration: 1 minute)** Heat olive oil in a non-stick skillet over medium-high heat. Wait until the oil shimmers, indicating it's ready for cooking. This step ensures that the meatballs will not stick and will have a golden exterior.
4. **Cook Meatballs (Duration: 4 minutes)** Add meatballs to the skillet, cooking in batches if necessary to avoid overcrowding. Cook for about 2 minutes on each side, until golden brown and cooked through. Turning them ensures even cooking and a delicious crust.
5. **Serve (Duration: 1 minute)** Arrange the cooked meatballs on a serving plate. Optionally, garnish with extra chopped parsley and serve with a side of tzatziki sauce for dipping. This presentation highlights the Mediterranean inspiration behind the dish, offering a visually appealing and tasty meal.

INGREDIENTS

- 1/2 lb (225g) ground turkey
- 1/4 cup (60g) breadcrumbs
- 1/4 cup (60g) feta cheese, crumbled
- 1 large egg
- 2 tablespoons (30ml) fresh parsley, chopped
- 1 tablespoon (15ml) olive oil
- 1 teaspoon (5g) dried oregano
- 1/2 teaspoon (2.5g) garlic powder
- 1/4 teaspoon (1.25g) salt
- 1/4 teaspoon (1.25g) black peppe

NUTRITION

- Kcal per serve: 375 kcal
- Carbohydrates: 10g
- Protein: 35g
- Total Fats: 21g
- Saturated Fats: 6g
- Monounsaturated Fats: 9g
- Polyunsaturated Fats: 3g
- Sodium: 580mg

Pork Tenderloin Medallions with Olives

1. Season Pork (Duration: 1 minute)
Season pork medallions with salt and pepper. Ensure each piece is evenly coated to enhance flavor. This preliminary step is crucial for developing a rich taste profile in the meat.

2. Heat Oil (Duration: 1 minute)
Heat olive oil in a skillet over medium-high heat. Wait until the oil is shimmering but not smoking. This ensures the pork will sear perfectly, locking in juices and flavor.

3. Cook Pork (Duration: 3 minutes)
Add pork medallions to the skillet. Cook for about 1.5 minutes on each side, or until golden brown. This quick sear ensures a tender, juicy interior with a flavorful crust.

4. Add Garlic and Olives (Duration: 2 minutes)
Reduce heat to medium. Add garlic and olives to the skillet, cooking for 1 minute. This infuses the dish with aromatic flavors and the salty tang of olives.

5. Finish with Broth and Lemon (Duration: 3 minutes)
Pour in chicken broth and lemon juice, and sprinkle with rosemary. Let simmer for 2 minutes, allowing the sauce to slightly reduce and flavors to meld. This final step creates a savory sauce that complements the tender pork beautifully.

INGREDIENTS
- 1 lb (450g) pork tenderloin, sliced into medallions
- 2 tablespoons (30ml) olive oil
- 1/2 cup (70g) olives, pitted and sliced
- 1/4 cup (60ml) chicken broth
- 2 cloves garlic, minced (10g)
- 1 tablespoon (15ml) lemon juice
- 1 teaspoon (5g) fresh rosemary, chopped
- Salt to taste (2g)
- Black pepper to taste (1g)

NUTRITION
- Kcal per serve: 495 kcal
- Carbohydrates: 3g
- Protein: 48g
- Total Fats: 32g
- Saturated Fats: 7g
- Monounsaturated Fats: 18g
- Polyunsaturated Fats: 4g
- Sodium: 720mg

Chicken Souvlaki Skewers

1. **Marinating the Chicken (Duration: 3 minutes)** In a large bowl, whisk together olive oil, lemon juice, minced garlic, dried oregano, salt, and pepper to create the marinade. Cut the chicken breast into cubes and add to the marinade, ensuring each piece is well coated. Let sit while you prepare vegetables, to briefly absorb flavors.
2. **Preparing Vegetables and Skewers (Duration: 2 minutes)** Cut red onion and bell pepper into chunks sized to match the chicken cubes. Thread the marinated chicken, onion, and pepper onto skewers, alternating between them. This not only adds color and flavor but also ensures a balanced skewer.
3. **Preheating the Grill or Pan (Duration: 1 minute)** Heat a grill pan or outdoor grill over medium-high heat. A properly heated grill ensures the skewers will cook evenly and get those desirable grill marks without sticking to the grates or pan.
4. **Grilling the Skewers (Duration: 4 minutes)** Place the skewers on the grill. Cook for 2 minutes on each side, turning once. The high heat quickly sears the outside of the chicken, locking in juices and creating a slightly charred, smoky flavor typical of souvlaki.
5. **Resting and Serving (Duration: 1 minute)** After grilling, let the skewers rest for a brief moment. This allows juices to redistribute, ensuring every bite is succulent. Serve hot, garnished with a sprinkle of fresh parsley and lemon wedges on the side for added zest.

INGREDIENTS

- **1 lb (455 g)** chicken breast, cut into cubes
- **2 tbsp (30 ml)** olive oil
- **Juice of 1 lemon (5 tbsp or 75 ml)** lemon juice
- **2 cloves** garlic, minced
- **1 tsp (5 g)** dried oregano
- **1/2 tsp (2.5 g)** salt
- **1/4 tsp (1.25 g)** black pepper
- **1/2 (100 g)** red onion, cut into chunks
- **1 (150 g)** bell pepper, cut into chunks

NUTRITION

- **Kcal:** 400 kcal
- **Carbohydrates:** 10 g
- **Protein:** 55 g
- **Total Fats:** 18 g
- **Saturated Fats:** 3 g
- **Monounsaturated Fats:** 10 g
- **Polyunsaturated Fats:** 3 g
- **Sodium:** 620 mg

Mediterranean Cheese and Charcuterie Board

1. Selecting the Board (Duration: 1 minute) Choose a large wooden or slate charcuterie board. Ensure it's clean and dry. This base will serve as your canvas, so its size is crucial to accommodate all your ingredients attractively.

2. Arranging the Meats (Duration: 2 minutes) Start by arranging the cured meats. Fold slices of prosciutto into halves or quarters, and roll or stack them neatly. Fan out slices of salami and chorizo for easy access and visual appeal.

3. Placing the Cheeses (Duration: 2 minutes) Add different cheeses to the board, spacing them out for variety. Cut some cheese into slices or cubes for immediate enjoyment, while leaving others in blocks for guests to cut into. This variety in shapes adds to the board's allure.

4. Adding Extras (Duration: 2 minutes) Scatter olives, nuts, and dried fruits around the cheeses and meats, filling in gaps. Place small bowls of hummus on the board. These elements add color, texture, and flavor contrasts.

5. Final Touches (Duration: 3 minutes) Fill remaining spaces with fresh vegetables and fruits. Add a basket or side plate with slices of crusty bread or pita. Ensure the board looks abundant and inviting. Every inch should offer a delightful mix of tastes and textures.

INGREDIENTS

- 4 oz (115g) assorted cured meats (prosciutto, salami, chorizo)
- 3 oz (85g) mixed olives
- 3 oz (85g) cheese assortment (feta, aged cheddar, gouda)
- 2 oz (60g) hummus
- 1 oz (30g) nuts (almonds, walnuts)
- 1 oz (30g) dried fruits (apricots, figs)
- 5 oz (140g) fresh vegetables (cucumber, bell peppers)
- 2 oz (60g) fresh fruits (grapes, berries)
- 4 slices (4 oz or 115g) crusty bread or pita

NUTRITION

- Kcal: 650
- Carbohydrates: 45g
- Protein: 25g
- Total Fats: 45g
- Saturated Fats: 15g
- Monounsaturated Fats: 20g
- Polyunsaturated Fats: 5g
- Sodium: 1800mg

Avocado and Crab Salad

1. **Mixing the Dressing (2 minutes)** In a small bowl, whisk together lemon juice, olive oil, salt, and black pepper until well combined. This dressing will add a zesty flavor to the crab and avocado, marrying the ingredients with a tangy richness.
2. **Preparing the Avocado (2 minutes)** Slice the avocado in half, remove the pit, and dice into small cubes. Place in a medium bowl. Drizzle half of the dressing over the avocado to prevent browning and gently toss to coat. This keeps the avocado vibrant and adds a layer of flavor.
3. **Adding the Crab (1 minute)** Gently fold the crab meat into the avocado mixture, being careful not to break up the crab too much. This step ensures each bite is a perfect blend of creamy avocado and sweet, tender crab.
4. **Final Touches (3 minutes)** Add the chopped cilantro and diced red onion to the crab and avocado mixture. Gently mix to distribute the ingredients evenly. The cilantro and onion will add a fresh and slightly spicy kick to the salad.
5. **Plating (2 minutes)** Arrange mixed greens on two plates. Top each with half of the crab and avocado mixture. Drizzle the remaining dressing over the salads before serving. The greens not only add color and texture but also balance the richness of the avocado and crab.

INGREDIENTS

- 8 oz (225g) crab meat
- 1 large avocado (200g after peeling and pitting)
- 2 tablespoons (30 ml) lemon juice
- 1/4 cup (60 ml) olive oil
- 1/2 teaspoon (2.5g) salt
- 1/4 teaspoon (1.25g) black pepper
- 2 tablespoons (30 ml) chopped cilantro
- 1/4 cup (25g) diced red onion
- Mixed greens for serving (2 cups or 60g)

NUTRITION

- **Kcal:** 485
- **Carbohydrates:** 12g
- **Protein:** 22g
- **Total Fats:** 40g
- **Saturated Fats:** 5g
- **Monounsaturated Fats:** 25g
- **Polyunsaturated Fats:** 10g
- **Sodium:** 975mg

Prosciutto and Melon Platter

1. **Prepare the Ingredients (2 minutes)** Slice the cantaloupe into thin pieces. Lay out the prosciutto, arugula, and shaved Parmesan cheese. Prepare a serving platter. This step sets the foundation for a visually appealing and delicious platter, ensuring all components are ready for assembly.
2. **Arrange the Prosciutto (2 minutes)** Gently arrange the prosciutto slices on the platter, allowing them to slightly overlap. The key is to create an inviting and artful presentation that will make the platter not only a feast for the palate but also for the eyes.
3. **Add the Cantaloupe (2 minutes)** Place the cantaloupe slices around and on top of the prosciutto. The sweet, juicy flavors of the melon will complement the savory, salty prosciutto, creating a perfect balance of flavors that is quintessential to this dish.
4. **Garnish the Platter (2 minutes)** Scatter the arugula over the prosciutto and cantaloupe. Drizzle the balsamic glaze across the platter in a zigzag pattern. This not only adds a touch of elegance but also introduces a tangy sweetness that enhances the overall flavor profile.
5. **Serve with Parmesan and Pepper (2 minutes)** Finish by sprinkling shaved Parmesan and fresh ground black pepper over the top. The Parmesan adds a sharp, nutty flavor, while the pepper provides a slight heat, rounding out the dish beautifully.

INGREDIENTS

- 4 slices of prosciutto (115 g)
- 1/2 cantaloupe melon (about 1 lb or 455 g)
- 1/2 cup of arugula (0.5 oz or 15 g)
- 1 tablespoon of balsamic glaze (15 ml)
- 1/4 cup of shaved Parmesan cheese (1 oz or 30 g)
- Fresh ground black pepper, to taste

NUTRITION

- **Kcal per serve:** 250 kcal
- **Carbohydrates:** 18 g
- **Protein:** 15 g
- **Total Fats:** 12 g
- **Saturated Fats:** 5 g
- **Monounsaturated Fats:** 4.5 g
- **Polyunsaturated Fats:** 1.5 g
- **Sodium:** 870 mg

Smoked Salmon and Cream Cheese Cucumber Bites

Step 1: Prepare the Cucumber (2 minutes)
Wash the cucumber and cut it into 1-inch thick slices. With a small spoon, gently scoop out the seeds from each slice to create a hollow space for the filling.

Step 2: Mix the Filling (2 minutes)
In a bowl, combine the softened cream cheese, chopped dill, lemon zest, and a pinch of black pepper. Mix until all ingredients are well incorporated.

Step 3: Assemble the Bites (3 minutes)
Spoon or pipe the cream cheese mixture into the hollowed-out cucumber slices. Cut the smoked salmon into small pieces that fit nicely on top of the cream cheese.

Step 4: Garnish and Serve (2 minutes)
Place a piece of smoked salmon on top of each cream cheese-filled cucumber slice. Garnish with a small sprig of dill or a little extra lemon zest if desired.

Step 5: Final Touches (1 minute)
Arrange the cucumber bites on a serving platter. If needed, season with an additional sprinkle of black pepper or a squeeze of lemon juice over the top before serving.

INGREDIENTS

- 1 large cucumber (about 1 lb or 450g)
- 4 oz (115g) cream cheese, softened
- 4 oz (115g) smoked salmon, sliced
- 1 tbsp (15g) fresh dill, chopped
- 1 tsp (5g) lemon zest
- Freshly ground black pepper, to taste

NUTRITION

- Kcal per serve: 200
- Carbohydrates: 6g
- Protein: 12g
- Total Fats: 14g
- Saturated Fats: 7g
- Monounsaturated Fats: 5g
- Polyunsaturated Fats: 2g
- Sodium: 600mg

Chickpea and Roasted Pepper Dip

1. **Gather Ingredients (1 minute)** Collect all the ingredients. Ensure the chickpeas are drained and rinsed, the roasted red pepper is chopped, and the garlic is minced. Preparation is key for a smooth cooking process.
2. **Blend Chickpeas and Peppers (3 minutes)** In a food processor, combine the chickpeas, roasted red pepper, olive oil, lemon juice, garlic, cumin, salt, and pepper. Process until the mixture is smooth, scraping down the sides as necessary.
3. **Add Tahini (1 minute)** With the processor running, add the tahini to the chickpea and pepper mixture. Blend until the tahini is fully incorporated and the dip has a creamy texture.
4. **Season to Taste (1 minute)** Taste the dip and adjust the seasoning with more salt, pepper, or lemon juice as needed. The balance of flavors should be harmonious, with a slight tang from the lemon.
5. **Serve (1 minute)** Transfer the dip to a serving bowl. Garnish with fresh parsley if using. Serve immediately with your choice of vegetables, pita bread, or crackers for dipping

INGREDIENTS

- 1 cup (about 240g) canned chickpeas, drained and rinsed
- 1 large roasted red pepper (about 1/2 cup or 120g), chopped
- 2 tablespoons (30ml) olive oil
- 1 tablespoon (15ml) lemon juice
- 1 clove garlic, minced
- 1/4 teaspoon (1.25ml) ground cumin
- Salt to taste (about 1/4 teaspoon or 1.25ml)
- A pinch of ground black pepper
- 2 tablespoons (30g) tahini
- Fresh parsley for garnish (optional, about 1 tablespoon or 15g chopped)

NUTRITION

- Kcal per serve: 250 kcal
- Carbohydrates: 22g
- Protein: 8g
- Total Fats: 16g
- Saturated Fats: 2g
- Monounsaturated Fats: 9g
- Polyunsaturated Fats: 4g
- Sodium: 300mg

Greek Yogourt and Fruit Cups

Step 1: Mixing the Yogurt and Honey (1 minute) In a bowl, combine the Greek yogurt and honey. Stir thoroughly until the honey is evenly distributed throughout the yogurt. This sweet base will complement the freshness of the fruit.

Step 2: Preparing the Fruit (2 minutes) Rinse the mixed berries under cold water. Hull and slice the strawberries if included. This step ensures that the fruit is clean and bite-sized, making it easier to enjoy with the yogurt.

Step 3: Layering the Cups (2 minutes) Begin to layer the yogurt mixture into two cups. Add a layer of granola over the yogurt, followed by a layer of mixed berries. The granola adds a crunchy texture that contrasts nicely with the creamy yogurt.

Step 4: Garnishing (1 minute) Sprinkle sliced almonds on top of the berries for an extra crunch. Garnish with mint leaves to add a refreshing aroma and a pop of color. These elements enhance the overall flavor and presentation of the cups.

Step 5: Serving (1 minute) Serve the Greek Yogurt and Fruit Cups immediately. Enjoy them as a healthy and refreshing breakfast or snack. The combination of creamy yogurt, sweet fruit, and crunchy granola is delightful.

INGREDIENTS

- 1 cup (240g) Greek yogurt
- 1 tablespoon (15g) honey
- 1/2 cup (120g) mixed berries (strawberries, blueberries, raspberries)
- 1/4 cup (30g) granola
- 2 tablespoons (30g) sliced almonds
- Mint leaves for garnish

NUTRITION

- **Kcal per serve:** 250 kcal
- **Carbohydrates:** 35g
- **Protein:** 15g
- **Total Fats:** 7g
- **Saturated Fats:** 1g
- **Monounsaturated Fats:** 3g
- **Polyunsaturated Fats:** 2g
- **Sodium:** 55mg

Tomato and Mozzarella Caprese

1. **Slicing the Ingredients (2 minutes)** Thinly slice the tomatoes and mozzarella cheese. Arrange them alternately in a circular pattern on a serving plate, slightly overlapping each slice with the next to create a beautiful pattern.
2. **Drizzling the Dressing (1 minute)** In a small bowl, whisk together the extra virgin olive oil and balsamic vinegar. Drizzle this mixture evenly over the layered tomatoes and mozzarella. Ensure every slice gets a bit of this delightful dressing.
3. **Adding the Greens (1 minute)** Tear the fresh basil leaves by hand and sprinkle them generously over the tomatoes and mozzarella. This not only adds a burst of flavor but also an appealing pop of color.
4. **Seasoning (1 minute)** Season the arranged slices with salt and freshly ground black pepper to taste. The seasoning should be just enough to enhance the natural flavors of the tomatoes and mozzarella without overpowering them.
5. **Serving (1 minute)** Once seasoned, the Tomato and Mozzarella Caprese is ready to serve. This dish does not require any cooking or additional preparation time, making it a perfect, quick, and refreshing meal.

INGREDIENTS

- 2 medium tomatoes (about 1 lb or 450g)
- 8 oz (225g) fresh mozzarella cheese
- 1/4 cup (60ml) extra virgin olive oil
- 2 tablespoons (30ml) balsamic vinegar
- 1/4 cup (about 0.5 oz or 15g) fresh basil leaves
- Salt, to taste
- Black pepper, freshly ground, to taste

NUTRITION

- **Kcal per serve:** 450 kcal
- **Carbohydrates:** 8g
- **Protein:** 22g
- **Total Fats:** 36g
- **Saturated Fats:** 16g
- **Monounsaturated Fats:** 14g
- **Polyunsaturated Fats:** 3g
- **Sodium:** 550mg

Greek Yogurt with Honey and Walnuts

1. **Gather Ingredients (1 minute)** Collect all the ingredients. Greek yogurt provides a creamy base, honey adds natural sweetness, walnuts offer a crunchy texture, and cinnamon gives a hint of warmth. This preparation ensures everything is at hand for a seamless cooking experience.
2. **Prepare the Yogurt (2 minutes)** Place the Greek yogurt into two bowls. Smooth the tops with a spoon. The yogurt serves as a blank canvas for the sweet and nutty flavors that will be added. This step is crucial for achieving the perfect base for our toppings.
3. **Add Honey (2 minutes)** Drizzle one tablespoon of honey over the Greek yogurt in each bowl. Ensure even distribution to sweeten every bite. Honey not only sweetens the dish but also adds a beautiful glossy finish that makes the dish visually appealing.
4. **Sprinkle Walnuts (2 minutes)** Evenly distribute the chopped walnuts over the honey-drizzled yogurt. The walnuts add a delightful crunch and nutty flavor, contrasting nicely with the smooth yogurt and sweet honey. This step introduces a necessary texture variation.
5. **Garnish (3 minutes)** Finish by sprinkling a pinch of cinnamon over each serving, if using. This optional step adds a warm, spicy aroma that complements the sweet and nutty flavors perfectly. Serve immediately to enjoy the freshness of each ingredient.

INGREDIENTS

- 1 cup (240g) Greek yogurt
- 2 tablespoons (30g) honey
- 1/4 cup (30g) walnuts, chopped
- A pinch of cinnamon (optional)

NUTRITION

- **Kcal per serve:** 200 kcal
- **Carbohydrates:** 18g
- **Protein:** 10g
- **Total Fats:** 9g
- **Saturated Fats:** 1.5g
- **Monounsaturated Fats:** 2.5g
- **Polyunsaturated Fats:** 4.5g
- **Sodium:** 45mg

Chocolate-Dipped Figs

1. **Prep the Figs (1 minute)** Wash the figs gently under cold water and pat them dry with paper towels. This step ensures that the chocolate adheres properly to the figs, providing a clean surface for dipping.
2. **Melt Chocolate (3 minutes)** Combine the dark chocolate and coconut oil in a microwave-safe bowl. Microwave in 30-second intervals, stirring in between, until smooth and fully melted. The coconut oil helps thin the chocolate for a sleek dip and adds a subtle flavor.
3. **Dip Figs (3 minutes)** Dip each fig halfway into the melted chocolate, allowing the excess to drip off. This step not only adds a luxurious chocolate coating but also a delightful contrast between the sweet fig and the rich chocolate.
4. **Cool (2 minutes)** Place the chocolate-dipped figs on a parchment paper-lined tray. Sprinkle with a pinch of sea salt if desired, adding a flavor contrast that enhances the sweetness of the figs and the depth of the chocolate.
5. **Serve (1 minute)** Allow the chocolate to set slightly, which takes about a minute. Serve immediately for a fresh and indulgent treat that combines the natural sweetness of figs with the richness of dark chocolate in a simple yet elegant dessert.

INGREDIENTS

- 6 fresh figs (6 figs)
- 4 ounces (115g) dark chocolate, roughly chopped
- 1 tablespoon (15g) coconut oil
- A pinch of sea salt (optional)

NUTRITION

- **Kcal per serve:** 300 kcal
- **Carbohydrates:** 45g
- **Protein:** 4g
- **Total Fats:** 14g
- **Saturated Fats:** 8g
- **Monounsaturated Fats:** 4g
- **Polyunsaturated Fats:** 2g
- **Sodium:** 20mg

Orange and Almond Salad

1. **Prep the Oranges (2 minutes)** Peel the oranges and slice them into rounds. Removing the peel and the white pith exposes the juicy flesh, enhancing the salad's visual appeal and ensuring a burst of fresh citrus flavor with every bite.
2. **Toast the Almonds (2 minutes)** Toast the sliced almonds in a dry skillet over medium heat until golden and fragrant. This step adds a nutty depth and a crunchy texture, providing a pleasant contrast to the soft, juicy oranges.
3. **Mix the Dressing (2 minutes)** Whisk together the olive oil, honey, and white wine vinegar in a small bowl. Season with salt and pepper to taste. This dressing combines the sweetness of honey with the acidity of vinegar, creating a balanced flavor profile.
4. **Assemble the Salad (2 minutes)** Arrange the mixed greens on a plate, top with orange slices, and sprinkle the toasted almonds over the top. The mixed greens serve as a fresh, crisp base, while the oranges and almonds add layers of flavor and texture.
5. **Dress and Serve (2 minutes)** Drizzle the dressing over the salad just before serving. Gently toss to ensure all components are lightly coated. This final step marries the ingredients together, resulting in a harmonious blend of flavors and textures.

INGREDIENTS

- 2 oranges (2 oranges)
- 1/4 cup (30g) sliced almonds
- 2 tablespoons (30ml) olive oil
- 1 tablespoon (15ml) honey
- 1 teaspoon (5ml) white wine vinegar
- Salt to taste
- Black pepper to taste
- A handful of mixed salad greens (about 2 cups or 60g)

NUTRITION

- **Kcal per serve:** 280 kcal
- **Carbohydrates:** 34g
- **Protein:** 6g
- **Total Fats:** 16g
- **Saturated Fats:** 2g
- **Monounsaturated Fats:** 10g
- **Polyunsaturated Fats:** 4g
- **Sodium:** 10mg

Quick Berry Sorbet

1. **(Blend the Ingredients) (2 minutes)** Combine the frozen berries, agave syrup, water, and lemon juice in a blender. Blend until you achieve a smooth consistency. It's crucial that all components are evenly mixed to ensure a uniformly smooth sorbet.
2. **(Adjust Flavors) (1 minute)** Sample the sorbet mixture to adjust the sweetness or tartness. You can add a little more agave syrup for sweetness or lemon juice for acidity, tailoring the taste to your preference while keeping it healthy.
3. **(Optional Freezing) (2 minutes)** If the sorbet's consistency is too soft, briefly freeze it. This step is optional and depends on your texture preference and the effectiveness of your blender at creating a firm sorbet.
4. **(Immediate Serving) (2 minutes)** Serve the sorbet right after reaching the desired texture to enjoy its optimal flavor and consistency. Immediate serving ensures the sorbet is consumed when it's most refreshing.
5. **(Add Garnish) (3 minutes)** Embellish the sorbet with a garnish of fresh berries or mint for an extra touch of flavor and visual appeal. This step enhances the sorbet with fresh elements, making it even more inviting.

INGREDIENTS

- 2 cups (480g) frozen mixed berries
- 2 tbsp (30ml) agave syrup (as a healthier alternative to honey)
- 1/2 cup (120ml) water
- 1 tbsp (15ml) lemon juice

NUTRITION

- Kcal per serve: 180 kcal
- Carbohydrates: 46g
- Protein: 1g
- Total Fats: 0g
- Saturated Fats: 0g
- Monounsaturated Fats: 0g
- Polyunsaturated Fats: 0g
- Sodium: 5mg

Pistachio and Apricot Bites

1. **(Combine Ingredients) (2 minutes)** In a food processor, combine pistachios, dried apricots, chia seeds, honey, and vanilla extract. Pulse until the mixture is finely chopped and begins to clump together, ensuring an even distribution of flavors and textures throughout.
2. **(Form the Bites) (2 minutes)** Using your hands, take small portions of the mixture and roll them into balls. Aim for each bite to be about the size of a walnut. This process not only shapes the bites but also helps to compact the mixture for better cohesion.
3. **(Chill to Set) (3 minutes)** Place the formed bites on a plate and refrigerate for a few minutes. Chilling helps the bites to firm up, making them easier to handle and enhancing their texture, providing a cool, refreshing taste upon consumption.
4. **(Prepare for Serving) (1 minute)** After chilling, arrange the bites on a serving dish. This step is about presentation, making sure each bite is placed for easy access and visual appeal, inviting immediate enjoyment.
5. **(Garnish and Serve) (2 minutes)** Optionally, garnish the plate with additional chopped pistachios or apricot pieces for a burst of color and flavor. Serve immediately, offering a delightful combination of nutty and fruity tastes in every bite.

INGREDIENTS

- 1/2 cup (65g) pistachios, shelled and unsalted
- 1/2 cup (90g) dried apricots
- 1 tablespoon (15g) chia seeds
- 1 tablespoon (15ml) honey
- 1 teaspoon (5ml) vanilla extract

NUTRITION

- Kcal per serve: 220 kcal
- Carbohydrates: 32g
- Protein: 5g
- Total Fats: 10g
- Saturated Fats: 1.5g
- Monounsaturated Fats: 5g
- Polyunsaturated Fats: 3g
- Sodium: 0mg

Ricotta and Berry Parfait

1. **(Mix Ricotta and Yogurt) (2 minutes)** In a bowl, combine ricotta cheese, Greek yogurt, honey, and vanilla extract. Mix until smooth and well blended. This base will create a creamy and flavorful foundation for the parfait, offering a delightful contrast to the fresh berries.
2. **(Layer the Parfait) (2 minutes)** Begin layering the parfait in two glasses. Start with a spoonful of the ricotta mixture, followed by a layer of mixed berries. The alternating layers of creamy ricotta and vibrant berries create a visually appealing and flavorful experience.
3. **(Repeat Layers) (2 minutes)** Continue layering the ricotta mixture and berries until the glasses are almost full. Ensure each layer is distinct, contributing to the parfait's texture and taste. The final layer should end with a generous amount of the ricotta mixture for a smooth finish.
4. **(Top with Granola) (1 minute)** Sprinkle granola over the top layer of the ricotta mixture in each glass. The granola adds a crunchy texture, contrasting the creamy and juicy components of the parfait, enhancing its overall appeal and providing a satisfying crunch.
5. **(Serve Immediately) (3 minutes)** Drizzle a little honey over the top for added sweetness and garnish with a few berries. Serve the parfaits immediately, allowing the flavors to meld slightly while ensuring the granola remains crunchy. Enjoy a fresh and indulgent dessert that's both simple and sophisticated.

INGREDIENTS

- 1 cup (250g) ricotta cheese
- 1/2 cup (120g) Greek yogurt
- 2 tablespoons (30g) honey
- 1/2 teaspoon (2.5ml) vanilla extract
- 1 cup (150g) mixed berries (strawberries, blueberries, raspberries)
- 1/4 cup (30g) granola

NUTRITION

- Kcal per serve: 350 kcal
- Carbohydrates: 38g
- Protein: 15g
- Total Fats: 16g
- Saturated Fats: 8g
- Monounsaturated Fats: 5g
- Polyunsaturated Fats: 2g
- Sodium: 125mg

The Art of Mediterranean Meal Prep

Step 1: Planning Your Meals
Start by planning your meals around seasonal produce and lean proteins. The Mediterranean diet thrives on the freshest ingredients, so look for what's in season in your area. Sketch out your meals for the week, incorporating a variety of colors and nutrients. Think about including a rainbow of vegetables, whole grains like farro or quinoa, and lean proteins such as fish, poultry, and legumes. Plan for versatility; for example, a batch of quinoa can be a side dish one night, part of a salad the next day, and then mixed into a soup.

Step 2: Shopping with Purpose
With your meal plan in hand, create a shopping list that prioritizes fresh, whole foods. Visit your local farmers' market or grocery store with a focus on finding the highest quality ingredients available. Remember, the Mediterranean diet emphasizes food's natural flavor, so opt for organic where possible and choose ingredients with minimal processing. While shopping, think about how each ingredient can be used in multiple dishes to maximize efficiency and reduce waste.

Step 3: Preparing the Basics
Dedicate a few hours at the beginning of the week to preparing the basics. Cook grains and legumes in bulk; roast, grill, or sauté a variety of vegetables; prepare a large salad that can last a few days; and marinate and cook lean proteins. Consider making a versatile dressing or two, like a lemon-olive oil vinaigrette or a yogurt-based sauce, to add flavor to any dish. These prepared components can be mixed and matched to create meals on the fly.

Step 4: Embracing Leftovers
In the Mediterranean, nothing goes to waste. View leftovers as an opportunity rather than an afterthought. A roasted chicken can become the protein in a salad, part of a hearty soup, or the filling in a wrap. Grilled vegetables can be enjoyed cold in a salad, blended into a dip, or used as a topping for whole-grain pizzas. Be creative and open to combining leftovers in new ways to keep meals interesting and nutritious.

Step 5: Making Mealtime Special
Meal prep isn't just about the food; it's also about the experience of eating. In the Mediterranean culture, meals are a time for relaxation and socialization. Even if you're eating alone, take the time to set the table, maybe light a candle, and truly savor each bite. This mindful approach to eating enhances the mealtime experience, making it more satisfying and enjoyable.

Seasonal Feasts: Eating with the Mediterranean Calendar

The Philosophy of Seasonal Eating
Eating with the seasons is a cornerstone of the Mediterranean diet, a pattern of eating that has captivated the world with its health benefits and delicious diversity. This approach is predicated on consuming fruits, vegetables, and seafood at their peak of freshness and nutritional value, ensuring meals are not only more flavorful but also more nourishing.

Spring: A Rebirth of Flavor
As the chill of winter recedes, the Mediterranean landscape bursts into life, offering a bounty of tender greens, artichokes, asparagus, and sweet peas. Spring is the time to rejuvenate your palate with dishes that reflect the freshness of the season. A simple fava bean and pecorino salad, artichoke risotto, or grilled asparagus with lemon and olive oil can capture the essence of spring on your plate. Seafood, too, welcomes the season with the arrival of fresh sardines and sea bream, perfect for grilling or baking with a medley of spring vegetables.

Summer: The Zenith of Sun-Kissed Flavors
Summer in the Mediterranean is a celebration of abundance, with markets overflowing with ripe tomatoes, peppers, eggplants, zucchinis, and a plethora of stone fruits and berries. It's a time for vibrant salads like the iconic Greek salad, refreshing gazpachos, and dishes that require minimal cooking, such as caprese with lush, ripe tomatoes and fresh mozzarella. Seafood dishes take on a lighter note, with grilled octopus, calamari, and a variety of fish perfectly complementing the season's produce. Embrace the tradition of outdoor dining, where meals are enjoyed under the sun or stars.

Autumn: A Harvest of Depth and Warmth
As the heat of summer gives way to the mellow warmth of autumn, the Mediterranean harvest yields a richer palette of flavors. Squash, pumpkins, mushrooms, and late-season grapes become the stars of the culinary show. This season calls for heartier dishes that reflect the gathering in of the harvest—roasted vegetables, mushroom risottos, and stews that simmer slowly, melding the flavors of autumn into comforting meals. Seafood like mussels and clams are at their best, lending themselves to rich, flavorful broths and pasta dishes that warm the soul.

Winter: A Time for Reflection and Nourishment
Winter in the Mediterranean might not be as harsh as in other parts of the world, but it's a season that speaks of introspection and gathering around the hearth. Root vegetables, cabbages, citrus fruits, and hardy greens dominate the table, offering sustenance and warmth. It's a perfect time for slow-cooked stews, braises, and soups that make use of the season's produce and dried legumes. Seafood, too, adapts to the season, with heartier fish like cod and sea bass featured in dishes that are comforting.

Stress Reduction: The Mediterranean Way to Wellbeing

Socializing as a Stress Reliever
Social connections are at the heart of the Mediterranean way of life. Meals are often communal, gatherings are frequent, and relationships are nurtured through face-to-face interactions. This emphasis on socializing is not just about enjoyment; it's a vital component of mental health. Social support networks provide emotional sustenance, reduce feelings of isolation, and have been shown to buffer the effects of stress. Incorporating regular social activities into one's routine, whether it's family meals, outings with friends, or community events, can help mimic this Mediterranean practice, fostering a sense of belonging and reducing stress.

Embracing the Outdoors
The Mediterranean lifestyle is closely tied to the natural world, with a strong emphasis on spending time outdoors. The region's climate facilitates a life lived in harmony with nature, where activities such as walking, gardening, and outdoor dining are woven into the fabric of daily life. The benefits of this connection to nature are manifold; sunlight exposure helps regulate sleep patterns and mood, while physical activity in natural settings has been shown to lower stress levels, improve mental health, and enhance physical wellbeing. To adopt this practice, look for opportunities to be outside each day, whether it's a walk in a local park, gardening, or simply enjoying a meal al fresco.

The Role of Physical Activity
Physical activity is a cornerstone of the Mediterranean lifestyle, seamlessly integrated into daily routines rather than segregated as a separate task. From walking and cycling as modes of transportation to dancing at social gatherings, movement is a natural part of life. Regular physical activity is a well-documented stress reducer, known to release endorphins, improve sleep quality, and reduce symptoms of anxiety and depression. Incorporating more movement into your day, in ways that are enjoyable and sustainable, can help you harness these benefits for stress reduction and mental health.

Mindful Eating for Mindful Living
The Mediterranean diet is as much about how you eat as what you eat. Meals are savored slowly, often shared with others, and approached with gratitude and mindfulness. This practice of mindful eating can extend beyond the table to foster a broader attitude of mindfulness—being fully present and engaged in the moment, which is known to reduce stress and increase contentment. To integrate this practice into your life, begin by focusing on the sensory experiences of eating, and gradually expand this awareness to other areas of your life.

Cultivating Creativity and Leisure
Leisure and creativity play significant roles in the Mediterranean lifestyle, offering outlets for expression, relaxation, and joy. Engaging in creative activities such as cooking, painting, music, or writing can be therapeutic, providing a respite from stress and an opportunity for self-expression. Likewise, leisure activities, whether they're hobbies, sports, or simply taking time to relax and do nothing, are essential for mental health. They provide a counterbalance to work and responsibilities, allowing for rejuvenation and perspective.

WEEK 1

Monday
- Breakfast: Greek Yogurt Parfait
- Snack: Classic Hummus with Veggie Sticks
- Lunch: Speedy Greek Salad
- Dinner: Garlic Lemon Shrimp

Tuesday
- Breakfast: Mini Frittatas with Spinach and Feta
- Snack: Caprese Skewers
- Lunch: Mediterranean Chickpea Salad
- Dinner: Lemon Herb Chicken Cutlets

Wednesday
- Breakfast: Mediterranean Avocado Toast
- Snack: Olive Tapenade on Crostini
- Lunch: Turkey and Hummus Wrap
- Dinner: Quick Pesto Zoodles

Thursday
- Breakfast: Banana and Nut Butter Roll-Ups
- Snack: Greek Yogurt Tzatziki with Cucumbers
- Lunch: Quinoa Tabbouleh
- Dinner: Sautéed Shrimp over Quinoa

Friday
- Breakfast: Quick Shakshuka
- Snack: Stuffed Dates with Almond
- Lunch: Grilled Vegetable Pita
- Dinner: Quick Sardine Pasta

Saturday
- Breakfast: Cottage Cheese with Pistachios and Honey
- Snack: Quick Marinated Olives
- Lunch: Falafel Wrap with Tahini Sauce
- Dinner: Salmon with Dill Yogurt Sauce

Sunday
- Breakfast: Greek Yogurt and Fruit Cups
- Snack: A Different Favorite from the Week
- Lunch: Arugula and Watermelon Salad
- Dinner: Mediterranean Turkey Meatballs

WEEK 2

Monday
- Breakfast: Mediterranean Avocado Toast
- Snack: Greek Yogurt Tzatziki with Cucumbers
- Lunch: Speedy Greek Salad
- Dinner: Quick Lamb Kofta

Tuesday
- Breakfast: Greek Yogurt Parfait
- Snack: Stuffed Dates with Almond
- Lunch: Quinoa Tabbouleh
- Dinner: Garlic Lemon Shrimp

Wednesday
- Breakfast: Mini Frittatas with Spinach and Feta
- Snack: Classic Hummus with Veggie Sticks
- Lunch: Mediterranean Chickpea Salad
- Dinner: Lemon Herb Chicken Cutlets

Thursday
- Breakfast: Banana and Nut Butter Roll-Ups
- Snack: Quick Marinated Olives
- Lunch: Turkey and Hummus Wrap
- Dinner: Sautéed Shrimp over Quinoa

Friday
- Breakfast: Quick Shakshuka
- Snack: Olive Tapenade on Crostini
- Lunch: Grilled Vegetable Pita
- Dinner: Quick Pesto Zoodles

Saturday
- Breakfast: Cottage Cheese with Pistachios and Honey
- Snack: Caprese Skewers
- Lunch: Falafel Wrap with Tahini Sauce
- Dinner: Salmon with Dill Yogurt Sauce

Sunday
- Breakfast: Greek Yogurt and Fruit Cups
- Snack: A Different Favorite from the Week
- Lunch: Arugula and Watermelon Salad
- Dinner: Mediterranean Turkey Meatballs

WEEK 3

Monday
- Breakfast: Banana and Nut Butter Roll-Ups
- Snack: Greek Yogurt Tzatziki with Cucumbers
- Lunch: Spinach and Avocado Salad
- Dinner: Quick Eggplant Parmesan

Tuesday
- Breakfast: Greek Yogurt Parfait
- Snack: Stuffed Dates with Almond
- Lunch: Tuna and Olive Tapenade Sandwich
- Dinner: Quick Sardine Pasta

Wednesday
- Breakfast: Mediterranean Avocado Toast
- Snack: Classic Hummus with Veggie Sticks
- Lunch: Cucumber and Feta Salad
- Dinner: Garlic and Herb Roasted Cauliflower

Thursday
- Breakfast: Cottage Cheese with Pistachios and Honey
- Snack: Quick Marinated Olives
- Lunch: Mediterranean Chicken Pita
- Dinner: Lemon Garlic Couscous

Friday
- Breakfast: Quick Shakshuka
- Snack: Olive Tapenade on Crostini
- Lunch: Quinoa Tabbouleh
- Dinner: Seared Tuna Salad

Saturday
- Breakfast: Mini Frittatas with Spinach and Feta
- Snack: Caprese Skewers
- Lunch: Grilled Vegetable Pita
- Dinner: Mediterranean Rice Salad

Sunday
- Breakfast: Greek Yogurt and Fruit Cups
- Snack: A Different Favorite from the Week
- Lunch: Arugula and Watermelon Salad
- Dinner: Pork Tenderloin Medallions with Olives

WEEK 4

Monday
- Breakfast: Mediterranean Avocado Toast
- Snack: Classic Hummus with Veggie Sticks
- Lunch: Speedy Greek Salad
- Dinner: Garlic Lemon Shrimp

Tuesday
- Breakfast: Banana and Nut Butter Roll-Ups
- Snack: Greek Yogurt Tzatziki with Cucumbers
- Lunch: Quinoa Tabbouleh
- Dinner: Sautéed Shrimp over Quinoa

Wednesday
- Breakfast: Cottage Cheese with Pistachios and Honey
- Snack: Stuffed Dates with Almond
- Lunch: Turkey and Hummus Wrap
- Dinner: Quick Pesto Zoodles

Thursday
- Breakfast: Greek Yogurt Parfait
- Snack: Olive Tapenade on Crostini
- Lunch: Mediterranean Chickpea Salad
- Dinner: Lemon Herb Chicken Cutlets

Friday
- Breakfast: Quick Shakshuka
- Snack: Caprese Skewers
- Lunch: Falafel Wrap with Tahini Sauce
- Dinner: Quick Sardine Pasta

Saturday
- Breakfast: Mini Frittatas with Spinach and Feta
- Snack: Quick Marinated Olives
- Lunch: Grilled Vegetable Pita
- Dinner: Salmon with Dill Yogurt Sauce

Sunday
- Breakfast: Greek Yogurt and Fruit Cups
- Snack: A Different Favorite from the Week
- Lunch: Spinach and Avocado Salad
- Dinner: Mediterranean Turkey Meatballs

WEEK 5

Monday
- **Breakfast:** Greek Yogurt Parfait
- **Snack:** Classic Hummus with Veggie Sticks
- **Lunch:** Spinach and Feta Orzo
- **Dinner:** Lemon Herb Chicken Cutlets

Tuesday
- **Breakfast:** Mediterranean Avocado Toast
- **Snack:** Caprese Skewers
- **Lunch:** Quick Marinated Olives & Arugula and Watermelon Salad
- **Dinner:** Quick Lamb Kofta

Wednesday
- **Breakfast:** Cottage Cheese with Pistachios and Honey
- **Snack:** Stuffed Dates with Almond
- **Lunch:** Turkey and Hummus Wrap
- **Dinner:** Garlic and Herb Roasted Cauliflower

Thursday
- **Breakfast:** Banana and Nut Butter Roll-Ups
- **Snack:** Greek Yogurt Tzatziki with Cucumbers
- **Lunch:** Mediterranean Chickpea Salad
- **Dinner:** Sautéed Shrimp over Quinoa

Friday
- **Breakfast:** Quick Shakshuka
- **Snack:** Olive Tapenade on Crostini
- **Lunch:** Cucumber and Feta Salad
- **Dinner:** Grilled Octopus Salad

Saturday
- **Breakfast:** Mini Frittatas with Spinach and Feta
- **Snack:** Quick Marinated Olives
- **Lunch:** Grilled Vegetable Pita
- **Dinner:** Quick Sardine Pasta

Sunday
- **Breakfast:** Greek Yogurt and Fruit Cups
- **Snack:** A Choice of Your Favorite Snack from the Week
- **Lunch:** Quinoa Tabbouleh
- **Dinner:** Mediterranean Turkey Meatballs

WEEK 6

Monday
- **Breakfast:** Greek Yogurt Parfait
- **Snack:** Caprese Skewers
- **Lunch:** Speedy Greek Salad
- **Dinner:** Salmon with Dill Yogurt Sauce

Tuesday
- **Breakfast:** Cottage Cheese with Pistachios and Honey
- **Snack:** Classic Hummus with Veggie Sticks
- **Lunch:** Spinach and Avocado Salad
- **Dinner:** Quick Eggplant Parmesan

Wednesday
- **Breakfast:** Mediterranean Avocado Toast
- **Snack:** Stuffed Dates with Almond
- **Lunch:** Turkey and Hummus Wrap
- **Dinner:** Garlic Lemon Shrimp

Thursday
- **Breakfast:** Banana and Nut Butter Roll-Ups
- **Snack:** Greek Yogurt Tzatziki with Cucumbers
- **Lunch:** Cucumber and Feta Salad
- **Dinner:** Pork Tenderloin Medallions with Olives

Friday
- **Breakfast:** Quick Shakshuka
- **Snack:** Olive Tapenade on Crostini
- **Lunch:** Mediterranean Chickpea Salad
- **Dinner:** Quick Pesto Zoodles

Saturday
- **Breakfast:** Mini Frittatas with Spinach and Feta
- **Snack:** Quick Marinated Olives
- **Lunch:** Falafel Wrap with Tahini Sauce
- **Dinner:** Seared Tuna Salad

Sunday
- **Breakfast:** Greek Yogurt and Fruit Cups
- **Snack:** A Choice of Your Favorite Snack from the Week
- **Lunch:** Arugula and Watermelon Salad
- **Dinner:** Mediterranean Rice Salad

WEEK 7

Monday
- **Breakfast:** Greek Yogurt Parfait
- **Snack:** Stuffed Dates with Almond
- **Lunch:** Lemon Garlic Couscous & Spinach and Avocado Salad
- **Dinner:** Mediterranean Mackerel Toast

Tuesday
- **Breakfast:** Banana and Nut Butter Roll-Ups
- **Snack:** Classic Hummus with Veggie Sticks
- **Lunch:** Quinoa Tabbouleh
- **Dinner:** Beef and Arugula Pita Pockets

Wednesday
- **Breakfast:** Cottage Cheese with Pistachios and Honey
- **Snack:** Olive Tapenade on Crostini
- **Lunch:** Speedy Greek Salad
- **Dinner:** Quick Berry Sorbet (as a dessert treat) & Grilled Vegetable Pita

Thursday
- **Breakfast:** Mediterranean Avocado Toast
- **Snack:** Greek Yogurt Tzatziki with Cucumbers
- **Lunch:** Cucumber and Feta Salad
- **Dinner:** Lemon Herb Chicken Cutlets

Friday
- **Breakfast:** Quick Shakshuka
- **Snack:** Caprese Skewers
- **Lunch:** Mediterranean Chickpea Salad
- **Dinner:** Quick Pesto Zoodles

Saturday
- **Breakfast:** Mini Frittatas with Spinach and Feta
- **Snack:** Quick Marinated Olives
- **Lunch:** Turkey and Hummus Wrap
- **Dinner:** Garlic and Herb Roasted Cauliflower

Sunday
- **Breakfast:** Greek Yogurt and Fruit Cups
- **Snack:** A Choice of Your Favorite Snack from the Week
- **Lunch:** Spinach and Feta Orzo
- **Dinner:** Salmon with Dill Yogurt Sauce

WEEK 8

Monday
- **Breakfast:** Greek Yogurt Parfait
- **Snack:** Stuffed Dates with Almond
- **Lunch:** Tuna and Olive Tapenade Sandwich
- **Dinner:** Mediterranean Turkey Meatballs

Tuesday
- **Breakfast:** Cottage Cheese with Pistachios and Honey
- **Snack:** Classic Hummus with Veggie Sticks
- **Lunch:** Arugula and Watermelon Salad
- **Dinner:** Quick Lamb Kofta

Wednesday
- **Breakfast:** Mediterranean Avocado Toast
- **Snack:** Olive Tapenade on Crostini
- **Lunch:** Quinoa Tabbouleh
- **Dinner:** Sautéed Shrimp over Quinoa

Thursday
- **Breakfast:** Banana and Nut Butter Roll-Ups
- **Snack:** Greek Yogurt Tzatziki with Cucumbers
- **Lunch:** Speedy Greek Salad
- **Dinner:** Garlic Lemon Shrimp

Friday
- **Breakfast:** Quick Shakshuka
- **Snack:** Caprese Skewers
- **Lunch:** Spinach and Avocado Salad
- **Dinner:** Quick Sardine Pasta

Saturday
- **Breakfast:** Mini Frittatas with Spinach and Feta
- **Snack:** Quick Marinated Olives
- **Lunch:** Grilled Vegetable Pita
- **Dinner:** Grilled Octopus Salad

Sunday
- **Breakfast:** Greek Yogurt and Fruit Cups
- **Snack:** A Choice of Your Favorite Snack from the Week
- **Lunch:** Cucumber and Feta Salad
- **Dinner:** Lemon Herb Chicken Cutlets

WEEK 9

Monday
- **Breakfast:** Greek Yogurt Parfait
- **Snack:** Olive Tapenade on Crostini
- **Lunch:** Quinoa Tabbouleh
- **Dinner:** Quick Sardine Pasta

Tuesday
- **Breakfast:** Cottage Cheese with Pistachios and Honey
- **Snack:** Classic Hummus with Veggie Sticks
- **Lunch:** Speedy Greek Salad
- **Dinner:** Garlic Lemon Shrimp

Wednesday
- **Breakfast:** Mediterranean Avocado Toast
- **Snack:** Stuffed Dates with Almond
- **Lunch:** Mediterranean Chickpea Salad
- **Dinner:** Lemon Herb Chicken Cutlets

Thursday
- **Breakfast:** Banana and Nut Butter Roll-Ups
- **Snack:** Greek Yogurt Tzatziki with Cucumbers
- **Lunch:** Turkey and Hummus Wrap
- **Dinner:** Sautéed Shrimp over Quinoa

Friday
- **Breakfast:** Quick Shakshuka
- **Snack:** Caprese Skewers
- **Lunch:** Grilled Vegetable Pita
- **Dinner:** Mediterranean Turkey Meatballs

Saturday
- **Breakfast:** Mini Frittatas with Spinach and Feta
- **Snack:** Quick Marinated Olives
- **Lunch:** Falafel Wrap with Tahini Sauce
- **Dinner:** Salmon with Dill Yogurt Sauce

Sunday
- **Breakfast:** Greek Yogurt and Fruit Cups
- **Snack:** A Different Favorite from the Week
- **Lunch:** Arugula and Watermelon Salad
- **Dinner:** Pork Tenderloin Medallions with Olives

WEEK 10

Monday
- **Breakfast:** Cottage Cheese with Pistachios and Honey
- **Snack:** Olive Tapenade on Crostini
- **Lunch:** Spinach and Avocado Salad
- **Dinner:** Quick Eggplant Parmesan

Tuesday
- **Breakfast:** Greek Yogurt Parfait
- **Snack:** Stuffed Dates with Almond
- **Lunch:** Cucumber and Feta Salad
- **Dinner:** Garlic and Herb Roasted Cauliflower

Wednesday
- **Breakfast:** Mediterranean Avocado Toast
- **Snack:** Classic Hummus with Veggie Sticks
- **Lunch:** Speedy Greek Salad
- **Dinner:** Lemon Garlic Couscous

Thursday
- **Breakfast:** Banana and Nut Butter Roll-Ups
- **Snack:** Greek Yogurt Tzatziki with Cucumbers
- **Lunch:** Mediterranean Chickpea Salad
- **Dinner:** Grilled Octopus Salad

Friday
- **Breakfast:** Quick Shakshuka
- **Snack:** Caprese Skewers
- **Lunch:** Quinoa Tabbouleh
- **Dinner:** Seared Tuna Salad

Saturday
- **Breakfast:** Mini Frittatas with Spinach and Feta
- **Snack:** Quick Marinated Olives
- **Lunch:** Turkey and Hummus Wrap
- **Dinner:** Quick Lamb Kofta

Sunday
- **Breakfast:** Greek Yogurt and Fruit Cups
- **Snack:** A Different Favorite from the Week
- **Lunch:** Falafel Wrap with Tahini Sauce
- **Dinner:** Mediterranean Rice Salad

WEEK 11

Monday
- **Breakfast:** Mediterranean Avocado Toast
- **Snack:** Greek Yogurt Tzatziki with Cucumbers
- **Lunch:** Spinach and Ricotta Stuffed Mushrooms
- **Dinner:** Quick Lamb Kofta

Tuesday
- **Breakfast:** Greek Yogurt Parfait
- **Snack:** Classic Hummus with Veggie Sticks
- **Lunch:** Tuna and Olive Tapenade Sandwich
- **Dinner:** Garlic and Herb Roasted Cauliflower

Wednesday
- **Breakfast:** Mini Frittatas with Spinach and Feta
- **Snack:** Stuffed Dates with Almond
- **Lunch:** Quinoa Tabbouleh
- **Dinner:** Lemon Herb Chicken Cutlets

Thursday
- **Breakfast:** Cottage Cheese with Pistachios and Honey
- **Snack:** Olive Tapenade on Crostini
- **Lunch:** Speedy Greek Salad
- **Dinner:** Sautéed Shrimp over Quinoa

Friday
- **Breakfast:** Banana and Nut Butter Roll-Ups
- **Snack:** Caprese Skewers
- **Lunch:** Grilled Vegetable Pita
- **Dinner:** Quick Sardine Pasta

Saturday
- **Breakfast:** Quick Shakshuka
- **Snack:** Quick Marinated Olives
- **Lunch:** Falafel Wrap with Tahini Sauce
- **Dinner:** Mediterranean Mackerel Toast

Sunday
- **Breakfast:** Greek Yogurt and Fruit Cups
- **Snack:** A Favorite Snack from the Week
- **Lunch:** Arugula and Watermelon Salad
- **Dinner:** Chicken Souvlaki Skewers

WEEK 12

Monday
- **Breakfast:** Cottage Cheese with Pistachios and Honey
- **Snack:** Stuffed Dates with Almond
- **Lunch:** Mediterranean Chickpea Salad
- **Dinner:** Quick Pesto Zoodles

Tuesday
- **Breakfast:** Greek Yogurt Parfait
- **Snack:** Olive Tapenade on Crostini
- **Lunch:** Speedy Greek Salad
- **Dinner:** Garlic Lemon Shrimp

Wednesday
- **Breakfast:** Mediterranean Avocado Toast
- **Snack:** Classic Hummus with Veggie Sticks
- **Lunch:** Cucumber and Feta Salad
- **Dinner:** Seared Tuna Salad

Thursday
- **Breakfast:** Banana and Nut Butter Roll-Ups
- **Snack:** Greek Yogurt Tzatziki with Cucumbers
- **Lunch:** Turkey and Hummus Wrap
- **Dinner:** Mediterranean Turkey Meatballs

Friday
- **Breakfast:** Quick Shakshuka
- **Snack:** Caprese Skewers
- **Lunch:** Spinach and Avocado Salad
- **Dinner:** Quick Eggplant Parmesan

Saturday
- **Breakfast:** Mini Frittatas with Spinach and Feta
- **Snack:** Quick Marinated Olives
- **Lunch:** Eggplant and Roasted Pepper Wrap
- **Dinner:** Salmon with Dill Yogurt Sauce

Sunday
- **Breakfast:** Greek Yogurt and Fruit Cups
- **Snack:** A Different Favorite from the Week
- **Lunch:** Quinoa Tabbouleh
- **Dinner:** Pork Tenderloin Medallions with Olives

WEEK 13

Monday
- **Breakfast:** Greek Yogurt Parfait
- **Snack:** Classic Hummus with Veggie Sticks
- **Lunch:** Mediterranean Rice Salad
- **Dinner:** Garlic Lemon Shrimp

Tuesday
- **Breakfast:** Mini Frittatas with Spinach and Feta
- **Snack:** Caprese Skewers
- **Lunch:** Tuna and Olive Tapenade Sandwich
- **Dinner:** Quick Eggplant Parmesan

Wednesday
- **Breakfast:** Mediterranean Avocado Toast
- **Snack:** Stuffed Dates with Almond
- **Lunch:** Quinoa Tabbouleh
- **Dinner:** Lemon Herb Chicken Cutlets

Thursday
- **Breakfast:** Banana and Nut Butter Roll-Ups
- **Snack:** Greek Yogurt Tzatziki with Cucumbers
- **Lunch:** Speedy Greek Salad
- **Dinner:** Seared Tuna Salad

Friday
- **Breakfast:** Cottage Cheese with Pistachios and Honey
- **Snack:** Olive Tapenade on Crostini
- **Lunch:** Spinach and Avocado Salad
- **Dinner:** Mediterranean Turkey Meatballs

Saturday
- **Breakfast:** Quick Shakshuka
- **Snack:** Quick Marinated Olives
- **Lunch:** Falafel Wrap with Tahini Sauce
- **Dinner:** Grilled Octopus Salad

Sunday
- **Breakfast:** Greek Yogurt and Fruit Cups
- **Snack:** A Favorite Snack from the Week
- **Lunch:** Arugula and Watermelon Salad
- **Dinner:** Pork Tenderloin Medallions with Olives

WEEK 14

Monday
- **Breakfast:** Greek Yogurt with Honey and Walnuts
- **Snack:** Smoked Salmon and Cream Cheese Cucumber Bites
- **Lunch:** Spinach and Ricotta Stuffed Mushrooms
- **Dinner:** Lemon Herb Chicken Cutlets

Tuesday
- **Breakfast:** Banana and Nut Butter Roll-Ups
- **Snack:** Classic Hummus with Veggie Sticks
- **Lunch:** Speedy Greek Salad
- **Dinner:** Quick Sardine Pasta

Wednesday
- **Breakfast:** Mediterranean Avocado Toast
- **Snack:** Caprese Skewers
- **Lunch:** Mediterranean Chickpea Salad
- **Dinner:** Garlic and Herb Roasted Cauliflower

Thursday
- **Breakfast:** Mini Frittatas with Spinach and Feta
- **Snack:** Stuffed Dates with Almond
- **Lunch:** Tuna and Olive Tapenade Sandwich
- **Dinner:** Mediterranean Mackerel Toast

Friday
- **Breakfast:** Cottage Cheese with Pistachios and Honey
- **Snack:** Greek Yogurt Tzatziki with Cucumbers
- **Lunch:** Quinoa Tabbouleh
- **Dinner:** Pork Tenderloin Medallions with Olives

Saturday
- **Breakfast:** Quick Shakshuka
- **Snack:** Olive Tapenade on Crostini
- **Lunch:** Falafel Wrap with Tahini Sauce
- **Dinner:** Seared Tuna Salad

Sunday
- **Breakfast:** Mediterranean Cheese and Charcuterie Board
- **Snack:** A Favorite Snack from the Week
- **Lunch:** Arugula and Watermelon Salad
- **Dinner:** Grilled Vegetable Pita

Made in the USA
Las Vegas, NV
07 April 2024